IRISH EMIGRANTS IN NORT

Part Four and Part Five

by David Dobson

CLEARFIELD

Part Four originally published
St. Andrews, Fife, Scotland, 1998

Part Five originally published
St. Andrews, Fife, Scotland, 1999

Reprinted, two volumes in one, for
Clearfield Company, Inc. by
Genealogical Publishing Co., Inc.
Baltimore, Maryland
2000, 2004

International Standard Book Number: 0-8063-4998-0

Made in the United States of America

IRISH EMIGRANTS IN NORTH AMERICA

Part Four

by David Dobson

IRISH EMIGRANTS IN NORTH AMERICA,
Part Four

ABRAHAMS, ABRAHAM, born in Ireland during during 1744, absconded from Hugh Bowes in Philadelphia on 28 June 1769. [PaGaz#2116]

ADAMS, HENRY, born in Ireland during 1781, a farmer, arrived in Waldboro, USA, late 1821 on the ship Lydia, Captain Adams. [USNA]

ALEXANDER, ISABELLA, formerly of Londonderry, late of Baltimore, USA, 1817. [PRO.PCC.prob.37/371]

ALEXANDER, ROBERT, born in Ireland during in 1766, an indentured servant who absconded from William Hembel and Henry Rice in Philadelphia in March 1785. [PaGaz#2862]

ANDERSON, THOMAS, born in Ireland during during 1750, absconded from George Bard in Leacock township, Lancaster County, Pennsylvania, in May 1769. [PaGaz#2110]

ANDERSON, WILLIAM, late of Portlanone, Ireland, sought in Philadelphia County, Pennsylvania, in May 1769. [PaGaz#2116]

ANDREWS, MARY, born in 1804, a spinster, arrived in Newport, USA, late 1821 on the ship Belle Savage, Captain Russell. [USNA]

ARCEDECKNE, ANDREW, born in Ireland during during 1681, a barrister, died in Jamaica on 17 August 1763. [Spanish Town g/s, Jamaica]

ARCHEACON, JOHN, an Irish tailor, an indentured servant who absconded from John Cotteinger, Chestnut Street, Philadelphia, on 22 April 1772. [PaGaz.#2263]

ARCHER, WILLIAM, born in Kilkenny during 1747, a hatter who absconded from Mathias Graff, a hatter in Lancaster, Pennsylvania, in February 1769. [PaGaz#2116]

ARMSTRONG, ELEANOR, born in 1746 near Armagh, emigrated to Philadelphia on the Newry Packet, Captain Robinson, in June 1771, absconded from William Evitt at the Sign of the Bible in Heart, Strawberry Alley, Philadelphia, on 18 October 1771. [PaGaz.#2260]

ARMSTRONG, JOHN THOMPSON, born in Trillick, County Tyrone, died on Holland Estate, Jamaica, on 26 August 1844. [St Thomas parish g/s, Jamaica]

ARMSTRONG, MARY, born in Ireland during during 1771, immigrated from Ireland in 1784, an indentured servant who absconded from Jacob Mytinger at the Sign of General Washington, Vine Street, Philadelphia, on 31 October 1785. [PaGaz#2894]

ASPILL, JOHN, from Londonderry to Philadelphia on the Faithful Steward, shipwrecked off the Capes of Delaware in January 1786. [PEH#100]

ATCHISON, THOMAS, born in Ireland during during 1763, an indentured servant who absconded from Valentine Himes in Pikeland, Chester County, on 30 October 1785. [PaGaz#2892]

BAKER, JOHN, born in Ireland during, an indentured servant who absconded fromThomas Laycock in Marcus Hook on 5 August 1784. [PaGaz#2828]

BARRY, GARRET, Montserrat, died in Cornwall, pro.1658 PCC

BARRY, JAMES, a free planter in St Kitts, pro.1659 PCC

BARRIE, MARY, born in Ireland during, an indentured servant who absconded from Matthew Irvin in Philadelphia, in December 1785. [PEH#92]

BASKIN, THOMAS, from Londonderry to Philadelphia on the Faithful Steward, shipwrecked off the Capes of Delaware in January 1786. [PEH#100]

BASSETT, EDWARD, Leighton Bridge, County Carlow, settled in Rideau, Canada, during 1820. [PAC:RG8.B22894]

BAXTER, KENNEDY, with his wife, arrived in Canada on the Commerce in August 1821, settled in Lanark, Ontario, on 1 September 1821. [PAO.MS154]

BEARD, JOHN, born in Ireland during during 1752, absconded from the armed schooner Delaware of Pennsylvania, in March 1777. [PaEP#331]

BEATY, JAMES, from Londonderry to Philadelphia on the Faithful Steward, shipwrecked off the Capes of Delaware in January 1786. [PEH#100]

BELL, JAMES, born in Ireland during during 1767, a farmer, arrived in New York late 1821 on the ship Robert Fulton, Captain Holdridge. [USNA]

BENNETT, EDWARD, Corporal of the Glengarry Fencibles, settled in Drummond, Ontario, on 16 July 1816. [PAO.MS154]

BENNETT, WILLIAM, arrived in Canada on the Commerce in August 1821, settled in Dalhousie, Ontario, on 1 September 1821. [PAO.MS154]

BERRY, ROSS, settled in Edwardsburgh, Ontario, on 29 December 1819. [PAO.MS154]

BERTRAM, HENRY, with his wife, arrived in Canada on the Commerce in August 1821, settled in Lanark, Ontario, on 1 September 1821. [PAO.MS154]

BERTRAM, WILLIAM, with his wife and three sons, arrived in Canada on the Commerce in August 1821, settled in Lanark, Ontario, on 1 September 1821. [PAO.MS154]

BIRDS, PATRICK, born in 1760, a blacksmith from Dublin, an indentured servant who absconded from John Patton in Salford Forge in Philadelphia on 25 July 1784. [PaGaz#2826]

BIRRY, JOHN, with his wife, son and daughter, arrived in Canada on the Mary Ann on 8 August 1817, settled in Beckwith, Ontario, on 4 September 1817. [PAO.MS154]

BISHOP, THOMAS, born in Ireland during during 1798, a clerk, arrived in New York late 1821 on the ship Dublin Packet, Captain Newcomb. [USNA]

BLAIR, ROBERT, born in Ireland during in 1684, died in Worcester, New England,in February 1775. [Penn.Ledger#6]

BLAIR, THOMAS, from Londonderry to Philadelphia on the Faithful Steward, shipwrecked off the Capes of Delaware in January 1786. [PEH#100]

BLOOMER, JOHN, former soldier of the 104th Regiment, settled in Drummond, Ontario, on 22 August 1816. [PAO.MS154]

BOHANNON, JOHN, born in Ireland during in 1760, an indentured servant who absconded from George Hoppler in Providence, Montgomery County, on 3 July 1786. [PaGaz#2928]

BOLTON, JOHN, arrived in Canada on the Betty and Mary on 20 August 1815, settled in Beckwith, Ontario, on 9 December 1815. [PAO.MS154]

BOURKE, NICHOLAS, second son of Edward Bourke of Colnelaugh, County Mayo, emigrated to Jamaica in 1740, died on 11 December 1771. [Spanish Town g/s, Jamaica]

BOYD, JOHN, with his two daughters, arrived in Canada on the Commerce in August 1821, settled in Lanark, Ontario, on 1 September 1821. [PAO.MS154]

BOYD, SAMUEL, with his daughter, arrived in Canada on the Commerce in August 1821, settled in Lanark, Ontario, on 1 September 1821. [PAO.MS154]

BOYD, SAMUEL, born in Ireland during during 1798, a farmer, arrived in Waldboro, USA, late 1821 on the ship Lydia, Captain Adams. [USNA]

BOYD, WILLIAM, born in Ireland during during 1793, a farmer, arrived in Waldboro, USA, late 1821 on the ship Lydia, Captain Adams. [USNA]

BOYLE, CHARLES, arrived in Newcastle, Delaware, from Londonderry on the brig Mary in November 1789. [Pa.Pkt, 5.12.1789]

BRADEN, WILLIAM, a laborer, an indentured servant, who immigrated from Ireland on the Favorite, master Robert Alcorn, to Philadelphia in July 1784. [PaGaz#2832]

BRADY, JOHN, born in Ireland during during 1798, a farmer, arrived in New York late 1821 on the ship Dublin Packet, Captain Newcomb. [USNA]

BRADY, MICHAEL, born in Ireland during during 1750, absconded from William Tucker in Trenton, West New Jersey, on 18 March 1769. [PaGaz#2109]

BRADY, MICHAEL, born in Ireland during during 1740, absconded from William Tucker in Trenton, West New Jersey, on 23 July 1769. [PaGaz#2118]

BRADY, THOMAS, born in Ireland during in 1803, a farmer, arrived in New York late 1821 on the ship Dublin Packet, Captain Newcomb. [USNA]

BRAIDEN, JAMES, with wife and son, arrived in Canada on the Commerce in August 1821, settled in Lanark, Ontario, on 1 September 1821. [PAO.MS154]

BRAIDEN, JAMES, jr., arrived in Canada on the Commerce in August 1821, settled in Lanark, Ontario, on 1 September 1821. [PAO.MS154]

BRANNAN, MICHAEL, Irish servant, absconded from Thomas Butler, Carlisle, Pennsylvania, in July 1775. [PaJ#1178]

BREAKY, WILLIAM, settled in Cavan township, Newcastle district, Ontario, on 17 June 1819. [PAO.MS154]

BRENNAN, WILLIAM, born in 1777, sons Andrew born in 1827, Daniel born in 1823, Gilbert born in 1840, Roger born in 1819, William born in 1821, and daughter Jane born in 1829, from Ballykilcline, Kilglass parish, County Roscommon, emigrated from Liverpool on 18 October 1847 on the Creole, Captain Rattoone, to New York, arrived there on 22 November 1847. [AH#22/339]

BRIAN, MATTHEW, emigrated from Dublin on the snow Nancy, Captain Reilly, on 17 March 1787 bound for Baltimore, landed at Little River near Machias on 14 July 1787 and later at Newbury Port on 31 July 1787. [PaGaz#2985]

BRIGHT, JAMES, late Sergeant of the Glengarry Fencibles, settled in Bastrad, Ontario, on 20 October 1819. [PAO.MS154]

BRIGHT, THOMAS, late Sergeant of the Glengarry Fencibles, settled in Drummond, Ontario, on 16 July 1816. [PAO.MS154]

BRIT, JOSEPH, born in Ireland during during 1765, an indentured servant who absconded from Jacob Walker in Radnor, Chester County, Pennsylvania, on 10 April 1785. [PaGaz#2863]

BROCKET, JOHN, from Londonderry to Philadelphia on the Faithful Steward, shipwrecked off the Capes of Delaware in January 1786. [PEH#100]

BROGAN, JOHN, late of the Prince of York's Chasseurs, settled in Bathurst, Ontario, on 7 October 1819. [PAO.MS154]

BROWN, HAMILTON, born in 1775 in County Antrim, died on 18 September 1843. [St Ann's parish g/s, Jamaica]

BROWN, JAMES, born in Ireland during during 1801, a farmer, arrived in Philadelphia late 1821 on the brig Rising Sun, Captain Prince. [USNA]

BROWNE, JAMES, arrived in Philadelphia from Londonderry on the brig Conyngham, master Robert Conyngham on 1 August 1789. [Pa.Pkt.11.8.1789]

BROWN, JOHN, born in Ireland during, arrived in America during 1789, an indentured servant who absconded from John Nicholson in Philadelphia in October 1789. [PIG#1208]

BRYAN, MARY, born in Ireland during, absconded from George Littell in Kent County, Maryland, on 16 July 1769. [PaGaz#2119]

BRYSON, ANDREW, from Bangor, County Down, transported to St Pierre to undergo enforced military service, later settled in New York around 1801. [PRONI#T/1373]

BUSH, THEOBALD, born in Ireland during during 1755, a seaman on the Freemason, a schooner formerly known as the Nancy, accused of piracy, in 1785. [PaGaz#2854]

BUCKLEY, MICHAEL, late a private of the Glengarry Fencibles, settled in Drummond, Ontario, on 16 July 1816. [PAO.MS154]

BURNS, MARY, from Londonderry to Philadelphia on the Faithful Steward, shipwrecked off the Capes of Delaware on January 1786. [PEH#100]

BURNS, THOMAS, arrived in Canada on the Eolies on 24 July 1819, settled in Beckwith, Ontario, on 21 December 1819. [PAO.MS154]

BUTLER, CATHERINE, born in Ireland during during 1751, absconded from James Patterson in Raphoe township, Lancaster County, Pennsylvania, on 9 July 1769. [PaGaz#2117]

BUTLER, POLLY, born in Ireland during during 1735, a servant who absconded from the sloop Jean, Captain Cook, in June 1765, which had recently arrived from Cork. [PaJ#1175]

BUTLER, WILLIAM, an Irish servant, absconded from Hugh Sidwell, East Nottingham, near Philadelphia, in May 1769. [PaGaz#2111]

BYGRAVE, WILLIAM, late of the Prince of York's Chasseurs, settled in Bathurst, Ontario, on 7 October 1819. [PAO.MS154]

CAIGA, JOHN, or WATSON, born in Ireland during, a thief sought by Thomas Smedley, a fuller in Williamstown, Chester County, Pennsylvania, in February 1785. [PaGaz#2858]

CAIN, MATTHEW, an Irish indentured servant and coachmaker, arrived in Philadelphia from Dublin on 1 June 1768, absconded from David Scott, Conegocheague, Cumberland County, Pennsylvania, on 22 May 1769. [PaGaz#2110]

CALA, THOMAS, born in Ireland during during 1767, an indentured servant who absconded from David Denny in Uwchland, Chester County, Pennsylvania, on 1 January 1785. [PaGaz#2848]

CALDWELL, MATTHEW, from Londonderry to Philadelphia on the Faithful Steward, shipwrecked off the Capes of Delaware in January 1786. [PEH#100]

CALHOUN, GUSTAVUS, from Londonderry to Philadelphia on the Faithful Steward, shipwrecked off the Capes of Delaware in January 1786. [PEH#100]

CALHOUN, THOMAS, from Londonderry to Philadelphia on the Faithful Steward, shipwrecked off the Capes of Delaware in January 1786. [PEH#100]

CALAUGHAN, JOHN, a brickmaker, an indentured servant, who immigrated from Ireland on the Favorite, master Robert Alcorn, to Philadelphia in July 1784. [PaGaz#2832]

CALIGHAN, PATRICK, an Irish indentured servant who absconded from James Gallion, Spis Utiae Church, Harford County, Maryland, in January 1775. [PaGaz#2405]

CAMACK, JOHN, born during 1799 in County Antrim, died on 3 May 1841. [St Ann's parish g/s, Jamaica]

CAMPBELL, DANIEL, born in Ireland during on 19 September 1730, settled in Schenectady, New York, as an Indian trader during 1754, militiaman of Albany County around 1780, died on 16 August 1802. [ANY.I.73]

CAMPBELL, MARY, an Irish indentured servant who was jailed in Chester, Pennsylvania, 1 November 1784. [PaGaz#2839]

CAMPBELL, SARAH, from Londonderry to Philadelphia on the Faithful Steward, shipwrecked off the Capes of Delaware in January 1786. [PEH#100]

CAMPIN, JOHN, a butcher and runaway servant who arrived on the snow Charlotte, Captain Gaffney, from Waterford, on 28 August 1774. [PaGaz.#2402]

CARBERRY, CHRISTOPHER, emigrated from Dublin on the snow Nancy, Captain Reilly, on 17 March 1787 bound for Baltimore, landed at Little River near Machias on 14 July 1787 and later at Newbury Port on 31 July 1787. [PaGaz#2985]

CARBERRY, JAMES, born in Ireland during during 1799, a farmer, arrived in New York late 1821 on the ship Dublin Packet, Captain Newcomb. [USNA]

CARDEL, FRANCIS, born in Ireland during in 1775, absconded from Samuel Harvey, tailor, 6 Spruce Street, Philadelphia, in April 1793. [PIG#1443]

CARLIN, JOHN, born in 1817, wife Honor born in 1807, Bridget born in 1829, Ellen born in 1838, and Mary born in 1840, from Ballykilcline, Kilglass parish, County Roscommon, emigrated from Liverpool on 19 September 1847 on the Roscius, Captain Eldridge, to New York, arrived there on 21 October 1847. [AH#22/339]

CARLYLE, ANDREW, arrived in Philadelphia from Londonderry on the brig Conyngham, master Robert Conyngham on 1 August 1789. [Pa.Pkt.11.8.1789]

CARRINGTON, JOHN, born during 1833, from Ballykilcline, Kilglass parish, County Roscommon, emigrated from Liverpool on 18 October 1847 on the Creole, Captain Rattoone, to New York, arrived there on 22 November 1847. [AH#22/339]

CARSON, JAMES, late of the Prince of York's Chasseurs, settled in Beckwith, Ontario, on 22 September 1819. [PAO.MS154]

CARTER, JOHN, born in Ireland during during 1763, an indentured servant who absconded from James McCabe in Chester Church, Queens County, Maryland, in June 1784. [PaGaz#2824]

CASSADY, FRANCIS, born in Ireland during during 1799, a laborer, arrived in Philadelphia late 1821 on the ship William and Jane, Captain Brown. [USNA]

CASSADY, PATRICK, born in Ireland during during 1796, a laborer, arrived in Philadelphia late 1821 on the ship William and Jane, Captain Brown. [USNA]

CASWELL, ANDREW, with his wife, 2 sons and 1 daughter, arrived in Canada via USA, settled in Drummond, Ontario, on 9 December 1815. [PAO.MS154]

CAVANAGH, ART MCGRIFFIN, transported from Wexford to Barbados in 1656. [Commonwealth State Accounts, Ireland, 441/110]

CAVANAGH, MICHAEL, born in Ireland during during 1760, absconded from John Righter, Lower Merrion township, Philadelphia County, on 2 March 1777. [PaEP#331]

CAVANAH, TIMOTHY, born in Ireland during in 1812, settled in Cherokee County, Georgia, by 1850. [1850 Census]

CAVENEY, LUKE, born in 1802, wife Mary born in 1808, sons Edward born in 1836, Luke born in 1838, Patrick born in 1831, Thomas born in 1833, and daughters Mary born in 1829, Anne born in 1841, and Catherine born in 1847, from Ballykilcline, Kilglass parish, County Roscommon, emigrated from Liverpool on 25 April 1848 on the Creole, Captain Rattoone, to New York. [AH#22/339]

CHAMBERS, JAMES, with his wife and son, arrived in Canada via USA, settled in Drummond, Ontario, on 25 November 1815. [PAO.MS154]

CHERRY, WILLIAM, born in Ireland during during 1764, arrived in Philadelphia on the Dublin Packet, Captain Alcorn, from Dublin in 1786, an indentured servant who absconded from John Longstreth in Warminster, Bucks County, Pennsylvania, on 15 June 1787. [PaGaz#2978]

CLACY, MARY, Irish servant, absconded from James Morison, wigmaker, New Dock, New York, on 29 April 1765. [PaJ#1172]

CLARK, JOHN, born in Ireland during in 1751, a skinner, absconded from Nathan Cook in Philadelphia in July 1769. [PaGaz#2120]

CLARK, ROBERT, late of the Prince of York's Chasseurs, settled in Bathurst, Ontario, on 7 October 1819. [PAO.MS154]

CLINE, WILLIAM, born during 1790, father-in-law of Patrick Kelly, from Ballykilcline, Kilglass parish, County Roscommon, emigrated from Liverpool on 13 March 1848 on the Channing, Captain Huttleston, to New York, arrived there on 17 April 1848. [AH#22/339]

CLINTON, ELEANOR, born in Ireland during, absconded from Thomas Pennington in Moreland Manor, Philadelphia County, Pennsylvania, on 4 April 1769. [PaGaz#2123]

COCHRAN, JAMES, born in the north of Ireland, settled in Sudbury, Chester County, Pennsylvania, before 1730. [ANY.I.199]

COGAN, THOMAS, born in Ireland during during 1749, absconded from James McSparran in Little Britain township, Lancaster County, Pennsylvania, on 10 August 1769. [PaGaz#2123]

COLGAN, MARGARET, born in 1782, daughters Honor born in 1818, and Mary born in 1820, from Ballykilcline, Kilglass parish, County Roscommon, emigrated from Liverpool on 13 March 1848 on the Channing, Captain Huttleston, to New York, arrived there on 17 April 1848. [AH#22/339]

COLGAN, PATRICK, born in 1804, wife Anne born in 1807, sons Bernard born in 1839, Michael born in 1843, William born in 1846, daughters Anne born in 1835, Betty born in 1841, and Mary born in 1832, from Ballykilcline, Kilglass parish, County Roscommon, emigrated from Liverpool on 26 September 1847 on the Metoka, Captain McGuire, to New York, arrived there on 30 October 1847. [AH#22/339]

COLGAN, PATRICK, born in 1811, wife Mary born in 1807, sons Michael born in 1828, Patrick born in 1839, daughters Anne born in 1840, Bridget born in 1835, and Margaret born in 1831, from Ballykilcline, Kilglass parish, County Roscommon, emigrated from Liverpool on 19 September 1847 on the Roscius, Captain Eldridge, to New York, arrived there on 21 October 1847. [AH#22/339]

COLLINS, EDWARD, arrived in Newcastle, Delaware, from Londonderry on the brig Mary in November 1789. [Pa.Pkt, 5.12.1789]

COLLINS, PATRICK, born in Ireland during during 1796, a fisherman, arrived in Newberryport, USA, late 1821. [USNA]

CONKLIN, GRAHAM, late of the Prince of York's Chasseurs, settled in Bathurst, Ontario, on 21 October 1819. [PAO.MS154]

CONN, HUGH, born around 1685 in Macgiligan, graduated from Glasgow University, emigrated to Maryland, died in Prince George County, Maryland, during 1752. [GG]

CONNELL, MORGAN, indented servant from Youghall, County Cork, to Maryland on the Increase, master Philip Poppleston, assigned to William Sharp in Talbot County, Maryland, 1677 [MHR Patents, Liber 20, fo.184]

CONNELL, PATRICK, born during 1770, a weaver, enlisted into the British Army in Stakestow, Roscommon, in 1804, discharged in 1817, settled in Dalhousie, Nova Scotia, during 1820. [PRO.WO.25#548]

CONNELLY, BRIAN, son of Juggy Connelly in Grelly, Navan, County Neath, in Cecil County, Maryland, pro. 16 April 1754 Maryland [will Liber 35, folio 379]

CONNOR, ARTHUR, from Lisburn, settled Talbot County, Maryland, pro.1 December 1721 Maryland [will Liber 22, fo.103]

CONNOR, JAMES, born in 1803, wife Honor born in 1804, son Martin born in 1826, from Ballykilcline, Kilglass parish, County Roscommon, emigrated from Liverpool on 25 April 1848 on the Progress to New York. [AH#22/339]

CONNOR, JOHN, born in 1810, (died at sea), wife Catherine born in 1820, from Ballykilcline, Kilglass parish, County Roscommon, emigrated from Liverpool on 30 September 1847 on the Jane Classon to New York, arrived there on 19 November 1847. [AH#22/339]

CONNOR, TERENCE, born in 1797, wife Mary born in 1812, son Thomas born in 1827, and daughter Mary born in 1836, from Ballykilcline, Kilglass parish, County Roscommon, emigrated from Liverpool on 19 September 1847 on the Roscius, Captain Eldridge, to New York, arrived there on 21 October 1847. [AH#22/339]

CONNOR, THOMAS, an Irishman, deserted the armed boat Lord Camden, Captain Edward York, in March 1777. [PaEP#331]

CORAN, JOHN, late of the Prince of York's Chasseurs, settled in Bathurst, Ontario, on 7 October 1819. [PAO.MS154]

COMAC, DAVID, born during 1810 in Ballymoney, Ireland, died in Skipton on 30 January 1850. [St Ann's parish g/s, Jamaica]

CONNOR, BRYAN, an indentured servant shipped from Kinsale to Barbados or the Caribee Islands 1679. [Council Book of the Corporation of Kinsale]

COSGROVE, FRANCIS, born in 1768, a shoemaker, enlisted into the British Army in Burr, King's County, in 1804, discharged in St John in 1818, settled in Dalhousie, Nova Scotia, during 1820. [PRO.WO.25#548]

COSTELLO, ELLEN, born in 1792, son John born in 1839, daughters Bridget born in 1831 and Mary born in 1829, from Ballykilcline, Kilglass parish, County Roscommon, emigrated from Liverpool on 18 October 1847 on the Creole, Captain Rattoone, to New York, arrived there on 22 November 1847. [AH#22/339]

COSTELLO, THOMAS, born in 1802, wife Mary born in 1803, sons Martin born in 1836, Michael born in 1834, Thomas born in 1842 and Patrick born in 1831, daughters Anne born in 1832, from Ballykilcline, Kilglass parish, County Roscommon, emigrated from Liverpool on 13 March 1848 on the Channing, Captain Huttleston, to New York, arrived there on 17 April 1847. [AH#22/339]

COUGHLAN, JOHN, indentured servant from Youghall, County Cork, to Maryland on the Increase, master Philip Poppleston, assigned to William Sharp in Talbot County, Maryland, 1677. [MHR Patents, Liber 20, fo.184]

CRAIG, GEORGE, son of Margaret Craig in Ballybet, Queens County, pro.5 January 1816 Baltimore County, [MHR.Liber 10, fo.102.]

CRAIGE, ROBERT, born in Ireland during during 1765, a mason, who escaped from Newtown Gaol, Pennsylvania, on 11 September 1784. [PaGaz#2833]

CROGHAN, PATRICK, born in 1819, brother John born in 1823, and sister Margaret born in 1821, from Ballykilcline, Kilglass parish, County Roscommon, emigrated from Liverpool on 19 September 1847 on the Roscius, Captain Eldridge, to New York, arrived there on 21 October 1847. [AH#22/339]

CULEGAN, PATRICK, born in Ireland during, arrived on the Sisters, indentured servant of Simon Cotlie at Brookland Ferry, Long Island, jailed as a runaway in Chester Jail on 6 September 1784. [PaGaz#2832]

CULEGAN, SIMON, born in Ireland during, arrived on the Sisters, indentured servant of Richard Roads, Gunpowder Falls, Maryland, jailed as a runaway in Chester Jail on 6 September 1784. [PaGaz#2832]

CUMIN, FRANCIS, born in Ireland during during 1801, a farmer, arrived in New York late 1821. [USNA]

CUNNINGHAM, MATTHEW, late private of the Glengarry Fencibles, settled in Drummond, Ontario, on 16 July 1816. [PAO.MS154]

CUTHBERT, JOHN, from Newtonbarry, Ireland, settled at Rideau, Canada, in 1820. [PAC:RG8.B22894/49]

DALEY, CHARLES, an indentured servant shipped from Kinsale to Maryland or Virginia in 1677. [Council Book of the Corporation of Kinsale]

DALEY, MICHAEL, born in Ireland during during 1800, a farmer, arrived in New York late 1821 on the ship Dublin Packet, Captain Newcomb. [USNA]

DALEY, ROBERT, born in 1799, enlisted into the British Army in Donegal in 1812, discharged in St John in 1818, settled in Dalhousie, Nova Scotia, during 1820. [PRO.WO.25#548]

DALTON, WILLIAM, born in Ireland during in 1748, absconded from Samuel Mendenhall in Concord township, Chester County, Pennsylvania, on 2 August 1769. [PaGaz#2122]

DAVENPORT, FRANCIS, born in Ireland during during 1751, absconded from Benjamin Verner in Lancaster township, Lancaster County, Pennsylvania, in August 1769. [PaGaz#2122]

DAVID, MICHAEL, born in Ireland during, absconded from Joseph Anderson near the Blue Bell, Front Street, Philadelphia, in July 1769. [PaGaz#2117]

DAVIS, JOHN, from Londonderry to Philadelphia on the Faithful Steward, shipwrecked off the Capes of Delaware in January 1786. [PEH#100]

DAVISON, JOHN, born in Ireland during during 1756, a barber and indentured servant who absconded from Philip Clampher in Philadelphia during 1775. [PaGaz#2405]

DEACE, MICHAEL, born in Ireland during during 1769, an indentured servant who absconded from John Bartholemew in East Whiteland, Chester County, on 3 June 1786. [PaGaz#2923]

DEFFLEY, MARY, born in 1787, George born in 1821, and James born in 1827, from Ballykilcline, Kilglass parish, County Roscommon, emigrated from Liverpool on 18 October 1847 on the Creole, Captain Rattoone, to New York, arrived there on 22 November 1847. [AH#22/339]

DEFFLEY, PATRICK, born in 1787, wife Mary born in 1792, daughter Bridget born in 1833, from Ballykilcline, Kilglass parish, County Roscommon, emigrated from Liverpool on 18 October 1847 on the Creole, Captain Rattoone, to New York, arrived there on 22 November 1847. [AH#22/339]

DELANEY, JOHN, arrived on the James Bailey on 15 June 1817, settled in Bathurst, Ontario, on 30 June 1817. [PAO.MS154]

DENNING, MATTHEW, born in Ireland during 1779, a farmer, arrived in Waldboro, USA, late 1821 on the ship Lydia, Captain Adams. [USNA]

DENNIS, HUGH, born in Ireland during 1765, an indentured servant who absconded from John Rowan in Salem on 23 May 1785. [PaGaz#2872]

DENNY, EDMUND, born in Ireland during 1749, a weaver, absconded from George Smedley in Williamstown, Chester County, on 6 April 1769. [PaGaz#2103]

DEVIN, JAMES, from Londonderry to Philadelphia on the Faithful Steward, shipwrecked off the Capes of Delaware in January 1786. [PEH#100]

DICK, DAVID, with his wife and 2 sons, arrived in Canada on the Mary on 20 July 1817, settled in Kitley, Ontario, on 9 September 1817. [PAO.MS154]

DICK, WILLIAM, with his wife, 3 sons and 3 daughters, arrived in Canada on the Mary Ann on 8 August 1817, settled in Kitley, Ontario, on 9 September 1817. [PAO.MS154]

DILLON, PATRICK, born in 1767, enlisted into the British Army in Tipperary in 1804, discharged in Newfoundland, settled in Dalhousie, Nova Scotia, during 1820. [PRO.WO.25#548]

DINMORE, ROBERT, from Londonderry to Philadelphia on the Faithful Steward, shipwrecked off the Capes of Delaware in January 1786. [PEH#100]

DONACHY, DANIEL, late private of the Glengarry Fencibles, settled in Drummond, Ontario, on 16 July 1816. [PAO.MS154]

DONALDSON, HUGH, late of the 6th Regiment, settled in Bathurst, Ontario, on 7 October 1819. [PAO.MS154]

DONLAN, MARTIN, born in 1815, from Ballykilcline, Kilglass parish, County Roscommon, emigrated from Liverpool on 19 September 1847 on the Roscius, Captain Eldridge, to New York, arrived there on 21 October 1847. [AH#22/339]

DONLAN, PATRICK, born in 1819, wife Anne born in 1820, from Ballykilcline, Kilglass parish, County Roscommon, emigrated from Liverpool on 18 October 1847 on the Creole, Captain Rattoone, to New York, arrived there on 22 November 1847. [AH#22/339]

DONLAN, PATRICK, born in 1787, sons Edward born in 1822, John born in 1811, Patrick born in 1820, and William born in 1831, daughter Margaret born in 1833, from Ballykilcline, Kilglass parish, County Roscommon, emigrated from Liverpool on 18 October 1847 on the Creole, Captain Rattoone, to New York, arrived there on 22 November 1847. [AH#22/339]

DONNELLAN, PATRICK, born during 1770, enlisted into the British Army in Roscommon in 1804, discharged during 1817, settled in Dalhousie, Nova Scotia, in 1820. [PRO.WO.25#548]

DOUD, EDWARD, born in Ireland during, an ostler, an indentured servant who absconded from John Merick in Salesbury, Bucks County, Pennsylvania, on 19 September 1784. [PaGaz#2833]

DOUGHERTY, JAMES, from Londonderry to Philadelphia on the Faithful Steward, shipwrecked off the Capes of Delaware in January 1786. [PEH#100]

DOUGHERTY, JOHN, born in Londonderry during 1763, an indentured servant who absconded from his master Thomas Procter, Walnut Street, Philadelphia, in November 1788. [PIG#928]

DOWDALL, HUGH, emigrated from Dublin on the snow Nancy, Captain Reilly, on 17 March 1787 bound for Baltimore, landed at Little River near Machias on 14 July 1787 and later at Newbury Port on 31 July 1787. [PaGaz#2985]

DOWDALL, LAURENCE, born in Ireland during 1659, a soldier in Flanders, then in Darien around 1700, settled in St Andrew's parish, Jamaica, Colonel of Militia, died on 30 January 1743. [Greenwich g/s, St Andrew's, Jamaica]

DOWNEY, PETER, an Irish runaway servant imprisoned in Salem Gaol, New Jersey, on 18 December 1786. [Pa.J#2129]

DOYLE, JOHN, with his wife and daughter, arrived in Canada on the brig John on 3 September 1815, settled in Beckwith, Ontario, on 9 December 1815. [PAO.MS154]

DOYLE, JOHN, born 1785 in Ireland, a laborer, arrived in New York late 1821 on the ship Dublin Packet, Captain Newcomb. [USNA]

DUDDLESTONE, ROBERT, born in Ireland during 1755, an indentured servant who absconded from Sam McCormick in Newton, Cumberland County, on 19 June 1785. [PaGaz#2882]

DUFFY, PATRICK, born 1790, enlisted into the British Army in Roscommon 1813, discharged in Fredericton, New Brunswick, 1818, settled in Dalhousie, Nova Scotia, 1820. [PRO.WO.25#548]

DUGAN, JAMES, born in Ireland during 1799, a farmer, arrived in New York late 1821. [USNA]

DUGAN, MARY, born in Ireland during 1796, arrived in New York late 1821. [USNA]

DUNBAR, WILLIAM, born in Ireland during 1764, a weaver and an indentured servant who absconded from William Whitehill in Leacock, Lancaster County, Pennsylvania, on 25 December 1784. [PaGaz#2851]

DUNGAN, JOANNA, born in Ireland during 1746, absconded from Thomas Ware, Burlington County, New Jersey, 12 March 1766. [PaJ#1215]

DUNN, JOHN, born 1776, enlisted into the British Army in Queen's County 1804, discharged in Fredericton, New Brunswick, 1818, settled in Dalhousie, Nova Scotia, 1820. [PRO.WO.25#548]

DUNN, MARY, an indentured servant, who immigrated from Ireland on the Favourite, master Robert Alcorn, to Philadelphia in July 1784. [PaGaz#2832]

DUNNING, LAWRENCE, born in Ireland during 1735, absconded from John Roberts in Lower Merion, Philadelphia, 4.6.1769. [PaGaz#2116]

EARLEY, ROBERT, born in Ireland during 1762, a schoolmaster and an indentured servant who absconded from Curtis Grubb, Cornwell Furnace, Lancaster County, Lancaster County, Pennsylvania, 29 May 1785. [PaGaz#2872]

EGAN, P., born in Ireland during 1793, a book-keeper, arrived in New York late 1821 on the ship Robert Fulton, Captain Holdridge. [USNA]

ELLIOT, JAMES, born in Ireland during 1753, absconded from Nicolas Dienl in Philadelphia 31.7.1769. [PaGaz#2119]

ELLIOT, JAMES, from Londonderry to Philadelphia on the Faithful Steward, shipwrecked off the Capes of Delaware in January 1786. [PEH#100]

ELLIOT, JAMES, born in Ireland during 1766, a baker and an indentured servant who absconded from John Cooper in Northampton, Burlington, New Jersey, on 14 March 1786.[PaGaz#2913]

ELLIOT, ..., former Lieutenant of the Royal Marines, settled in Bastard, Ontario, 29.9.1819. [PAO.MS154]

ENGLISH, JOHN, former soldier of the Glengarry Regiment, settled in Drummond, Ontario, 22.8.1816. [PAO.MS154]

ENGLISH, JOHN, late of the 104th Regiment, settled in Burgess, Ontario, 22.8.1816. [PAO.MS154]

EWING, THOMAS, from Belfast, resident in Baltimore Town, Maryland, pro.11.4.1776. [Baltimore County Will, Liber 3, fo.402]

FAGAN, WILLIAM, an Irish tailor who absconded from Edward Scanlow and Charles Allen in Chestertown, Maryland, 16.8.1772. [PaGaz.#2280]

FAIR, ALEXANDER, settled in Cavan township, Newcastle district, Ontario, 15.2.1818. [PAO.MS154]

FALKNER, JAMES, born in Ireland during 1811, settled in Cherokee County, Georgia, by 1850. [1850 Census]

FALLON, GARRET, born 1815, wife Eliza born 1821, sister Bridget born 1827, from Ballykilcline, Kilglass parish, County Roscommon, emigrated from Liverpool on 18 October 1847 on the Creole, Captain Rattoone, to New York, arrived there 22 November 1847. [AH#22/339]

FALLON, THOMAS, born 1814, wife Anne born 1815, son Martin born 1842, daughters Ellen born 1839 and Mary born 1846, Patrick (Thomas's brother) born 1831, and Bridget (Thomas's sister) born 1822, from Ballykilcline, Kilglass parish, County Roscommon, emigrated from Liverpool on 18 October 1847 on the Creole, Captain Rattoone, to New York, arrived there 22 November 1847. [AH#22/339]

FALLON, THOMAS, born 1804, wife Mary born 1829, from Ballykilcline, Kilglass parish, County Roscommon, emigrated from Liverpool on 18 October 1847 on the Creole, Captain Rattoone, to New York, arrived there 22 November 1847. [AH#22/339]

FARMER, JAMES, born in Ireland during 1800, a farmer, arrived in Waldboro, USA, late 1821 on the ship Lydia, Captain Adams. [USNA]

FARRELL, BRIDGET, born 1812, from Ballykilcline, Kilglass parish, County Roscommon, emigrated from Liverpool on 13 March 1848 on the Channing, Captain Huttleston, to New York, arrived there 17 March 1848. [AH#22/339]

FARRELL, PATRICK, born 1793, wife Mary born 1798, son William born 1830, daughters Bridget born 1834 and Mary born 1832, from Ballykilcline, Kilglass parish, County Roscommon, emigrated from Liverpool on 13 March 1848 on the Channing, Captain Huttleston, to New York, arrived there 17 March 1848. [AH#22/339]

FELAN, SUSAN, an Irish servant girl, absconded from John Van Dren in Roxborough Mills, Pennsylvania, 31 August 1784. [PaGaz#2830]

FERGUSON, THOMAS, emigrated from Northern Ireland to Carolina 11 July 1684. [SPAWI#1684/1801]

FIELD, JAMES, born 1749 in Dublin, absconded from David Llewellyn, Pencader Hundred, New Castle County, May 1769. [PaGaz#2110]

FIELD, THOMAS, an Irish indentured servant who absconded from his master R. Hutchison in Charleston, South Carolina, in May 1734. [SCGaz#17]

FINLAH, ALEXANDER, born in 1744, an Irish indentured servant who absconded from John Rankin, New Garden township, Chester County, Pennsylvamia, in April 1772. [PaGaz.#2260]

FINLAY, THOMAS, arrived in Canada on the Mary Ann Bell on 9 July 1817, settled in Burgess, Ontario, on 15 August 1817. [PAO.MS154]

FINLAY, RICHARD, with his wife, 2 sons and 2 daughters, arrived in Canada on the Mary Ann Bell on 9 July 1817, settled in Burgess, Ontario, on 15 August 1817. [PAO.MS154]

FINN, PATRICK, born 1812, wife Margaret born 1823, Michael (brother of Patrick) born 1825, Bridget (sister of Patrick) born 1827, and Margaret (sister of Patrick) born 1838, from Ballykilcline, Kilglass parish, County Roscommon, emigrated from Liverpool on 26 September 1847 on the Metoka, Captain McGuire, to New York, arrived there 30 October 1847. [AH#22/339]

FINNEGAN, JAMES, a laborer, an indentured servant, who immigrated from Ireland on the Favourite, master Robert Alcorn, to Philadelphia in July 1784. [PaGaz#2832]

FISHER, GEORGE, born 1745, a runaway servant from Hasael Thomas, Vincent township, Chester County, on 1 January 1775. [PaGaz.#2405]

FITZBULARD, DAVID, born in Ireland during 1820, settled in Cherokee County, Georgia, by 1850. [1850 Census]

FITZGERALD, E., born in Ireland during 1810, settled in Cherokee County, Georgia, by 1850. [1850 Census]

FITZGERALD, EDWARD, born in Ireland during 1813, settled in Cherokee County, Georgia, by 1850. [1850 Census]

FITZGERALD, NICHOLAS, born in Ireland during 1745, absconded from Samuel Henry in Philadelphia on 13 August 1769. [PaGaz#2122]

FITZPATRICK, P., born in Ireland during 1799, a farmer, arrived in Waldboro, USA, late 1821 on the ship Lydia, Captain Adams. [USNA]

FLAUGHERTY, JOHN, born 1747 in Ireland, absconded from John Hannum in East Bradford, Chester County, Pennsylvania, on 1 January 1772. [PaGaz#2246]

FLEMING, DAVID, from Dublin, a merchant and soap boiler in New York, Freeman of New York on 5 May 1762, died 1762. [ANY.I.90]

FLETCHER, EDWARD, born in Ireland during 1773, a farmer, arrived in Waldboro, USA, late 1821 on the ship Lydia, Captain Adams. [USNA]

FLYNN, ARCHIBALD, arrived in Canada on the Betty and Mary on 20 August 1815, settled in Beckwith, Ontario, on 9 December 1815. [PAO.MS154]

FLYNN, JAMES, arrived in Canada via USA, settled in Bathurst, Ontario, on 9 December 1815. [PAO.MS154]

FOLEY, JOHN, late of the Glengarry Fencibles, settled in Bathurst, Ontario, on 23 July 1816. [PAO.MS154]

FOLEY, JOHN, with his wife, 3 sons and 2 daughters, arrived in Canada on the Active on 8 August 1817, settled in Yonge, Ontario, on 12 September 1817. [PAO.MS154]

FORSYTH, ELIJAH, from Baltenugh parish, County Derry, settled in America in 1771. [PaGaz#2826]

FORSYTH, JOHN, from Baltenugh parish, County Derry, settled in America in 1771. [PaGaz#2826]

FORSYTH, WILLIAM, from Baltenugh parish, County Derry, settled in America during 1783. [PaGaz#2826]

FORSYTH, JOHN, born in Ireland during 1791, a weaver, and his wife Catherine born in Ireland during 1794, and 4 children, arrived in Oswegatchie, USA, late 1821 on the boat Huron, master Graham. [USNA]

FOSTER, DAVID, born in Ireland during 1750, an indentured servant who absconded from Andrew Moynihan, breeches maker, Taylor's Alley, Second Street, Philadelphia, in August 1772. [Pa.Gaz.#2278]

FOX, JAMES, arrived in Canada on the Commerce on 16 September 1815, settled in Beckwith, Ontario, on 9 December 1815. [PAO.MS154]

FOX, FRANCIS, born 1813, wife Mary born 1815, sons Francis born 1844 and Patrick born 1841, Thomas (brother of Francis) born 1822, and Catherine (sister of Francis) born 1832, from Ballykilcline, Kilglass parish, County Roscommon, emigrated from Liverpool on 26 September 1847 on the Metoka Captain McGuire, to New York, arrived there 30 October 1847. [AH#22/339]

FRENCH, PATRICK, a Scots-Irishman, admitted as a member of the Scots Charitable Society of Boston 1716. [NEHGS/SCSpp]

GALLAGHER, MICHAEL, born 1823, sister Margaret born 1827, from Ballykilcline, Kilglass parish, County Roscommon, emigrated from Liverpool on 26 September 1847 on the Metoka, Captain McGuire, to New York, arrived there 30 October 1847. [AH#22/339]

GALLAHER, FRANCIS, born in Ireland during, late of the 1st Pennsylvania Battalion recently from Ticonderoga, absconded from a Pennsylvania armed boat, in March 1777. [PaEP#331]

GALLOWAY, ANDREW, emigrated from Top Mill, Ballimony, County Antrim, to Philadelphia on the Hannah from Londonderry in 1774. [PaGaz#2831]

GALLOWAY, JOHN, emigrated from Top Mill, Ballimony, County Antrim, to Philadelphia, by 4 September 1784. [PaGaz#2831]

GAMBLE, JOHN, second son of John Gamble a farmer in Bangor, County Down, matriculated at Glasgow University 1797, Secession minister in Clenanees, emigrated to America. [GG#183]

GARDLEY, JOHN, born in Ireland during 1774, settled in Cherokee County, Georgia, by 1850. [1850 Census]

GARRETT, EDWIN, born in Ireland during 1804, a gentleman, arrived in New York late 1821 on the ship Dublin Packet, Captain Newcomb. [USNA]

GARRETT, FREDERICK, born in Ireland during 1802, a gentleman, arrived in New York late 1821 on the ship Dublin Packet, Captain Newcomb. [USNA]

GARRETT, JOSEPH, born in Ireland during 1796, a gentleman, arrived in New York late 1821 on the ship Dublin Packet, Captain Newcomb. [USNA]

GARVIN, JAMES, former Corporal of the Royal Artillery, with his wife and son, settled in Drummond, Ontario, on 1 November 1816. [PAO.MS154]

GERRARD, MARGARET, indentured servant from Youghall, County Cork, to Maryland on the Increase, master Philip Poppleston, assigned to William Sharp in Talbot County, Maryland, 1677 [MHR Patents, Liber 20, fo.184]

GILES, HENRY, and wife, arrived in Canada on the Mary Ann on 8 August 1817, settled in Landsdown, Ontario, on 9 September 1817. [PAO.MS154]

GILES, MARK, born in Ireland during 1759, a runaway indentured servant jailed in Newton, Bucks County, on 13 October 1785. [PaGaz#2891]

GILL, BERNARD, born 1818, wife Catherine born 1823, sons Andrew born 1845 and Patrick born 1846, from Ballykilcline, Kilglass parish, County Roscommon, emigrated from Liverpool on 13 March 1848 on the Channing, Captain Huttleston, to New York, arrived there 17 April 1848. [AH#22/339]

GILLEN, JAMES, settled in Madue township, Merland district, Ontario, on 7 October 1818. [PAO.MS154]

GILLESPIE, JOHN, possibly from Clougher parish, County Tyrone, settled in Frederick County, Maryland, pro. Md. [MHR.will liber 36, fo.673]

GILMORE, ARTHUR HILL, emigrated from Dublin on the snow Nancy, Captain Reilly, on 17 March 1787 bound for Baltimore, landed at Little River near Machias on 14 July 1787 and later at Newbury Port on 31 July 1787. [PaGaz#2985]

GILLMORE, DAVID, born 1752, an Irish indentured servant who arrived in Philadelphia with Captain McCutcheon in the Fall 1771, absconded from John Moody at the Sign of the Death of a Fox, Chestnut Street, Philadelphia, on 25 January 1772. [PaGaz.#2260]

GINTY, MARGARET, born 1787, son Bernard born 1833 and daughter Bridget born 1831, from Ballykilcline, Kilglass parish, County Roscommon, emigrated from Liverpool on 26 September 1847 on the Metoka, Captain McGuire, to New York, arrived there 30 October 1847. [AH#22/339]

GLASSHAM, JOHN, born 1751, an Irish servant who absconded from John Evans and Joseph Jenkins, Carnarvon township, Lancaster County, Pennsylvania, in August 1772. [PaGaz.#2278]

GODFREY, EDWARD, an Irish indentured servant who absconded from Azariah Thomas, West Nantmell township, Chester County, Pennsylvania, in February 1772. [PaGaz.#2263]

GOODALL, SAUNDERS, with his wife and daughter, arrived in Canada on the Mary and Betty on 20 August 1815, settled in Drummond, Ontario, on 31 December 1815. [PAO.MS154]

GORMLEY, JAMES, born in County Tyrone, pro.21 January 1839 Baltimore County [will Liber 17, fo.205]

GRADY, NEIL, late of the Prince of York's Chasseurs, and his wife, settled in Bathurst, Ontario, on 7 October 1819. [PAO.MS154]

GRAHAM, EDWARD, born in Ireland during 1766, a tailor and indentured servant who absconded from William Hembel and Henry Rice in Philadelphia in March 1785. [PaGaz#2862]

GRAHAM, GEORGE, arrived in Canada via USA, settled in Bathurst, Ontario, on 31 January 1817. [PAO.MS154]

GRAHAM, JOHN, son of Francis Graham in Cavanallee, Strabane, County Tyrone, pro.18 April 1759 Maryland [Will Liber 30, fol.732]

GREEN, EDWARD, born in Ireland during 1796, a bookbinder, arrived in Philadelphia late 1821 on the brig Jane, Captain Richard. [USNA]

GREENE, JAMES, with his wife and 2 daughters, arrived in Canada on the Commerce on 16 September 1815, settled in Beckwith, Ontario, on 9 December 1815. [PAO.MS154]

GREENE, Mrs, daughter of the late Walter Thom, Dublin, died on passage to Quebec 1832. [AJ#4432]

GREGORY, JAMES, with his wife and 3 daughters, arrived in Canada on the Sally and Tom, settled in Edwardsburgh, Ontario, on 5 August 1817. [PAO.MS154]

GREGORY, SAMUEL, arrived in Canada on the Sally and Tom, settled in Edwardsburgh, Ontario, on 5 August 1817. [PAO.MS154]

GUNSHAN, FELIX, a shoemaker, runaway from the Faithful Steward of Londonderry in Philadelphia 31 August 1784. [PaGaz#2830]

HACKETT, THOMAS, born 1792, enlisted into the British Army in King's County 1816, discharged in Fredericton, New Brunswick, 1818, settled in Dalhousie, Nova Scotia, 1820. [PRO.WO.25#548]

HAGARTREE, PATRICK, born in Ireland during 1803, settled in Cherokee County, Georgia, by 1850. [1850 Census]

HALEY, WILLIAM, with his wife and 3 sons, arrived in Canada via USA, settled in Drummond, Ontario, on 31 January 1817. [PAO.MS154]

HALL, NICHOLAS, Private of the Glengarry Fencibles, settled in Drummond, Ontario, on 16 July 1816. [PAO.MS154]

HALLARD, ANDREW, late from the Isle of Bart, County Donegal, sought by his brother John Hallard, Sasquhanna Lower Ferry, Cecil County, Maryland, in January 1772. [PaGaz#2247]

HAMILTON, RICHARD, arrived in Newcastle, Delaware, from Londonderry on the brig Mary in November 1789. [Pa.Pkt, 5.12.1789]

HANLEN, MATTHEW, born in Ireland during 1798, a farmer, arrived in New York late 1821 on the ship Dublin Packet, Captain Newcomb. [USNA]

HANLEY, HUGH, born in Ireland during, arrived on the Sisters, indentured servant of Thomas McKinn in Philadelphia, jailed as a runaway in Chester Jail on 6 September 1784. [PaGaz#2832]

HANLEY, JAMES, born 1783, wife Betty born 1793, sons James born 1833, John born 1829, Martin born 1825, Patrick born 1827, Roger born 1835, and Mary born 1830, from Ballykilcline, Kilglass parish, County Roscommon, emigrated from Liverpool on 26 September 1847 on the Channing, Captain Huttleston, to New York, arrived there 30 September 1847. [AH#22/339]

HANLEY, JAMES, born 1817, wife Susan born 1817, sons John born 1840 and Peter born 1842, from Ballykilcline, Kilglass parish, County Roscommon, emigrated from Liverpool on 18 October 1847 on the Creole, Captain Rattoone, to New York, arrived there 22 November 1847. [AH#22/339]

HANLEY, THOMAS, born 1787, wife Mary born 1797, sons Darby born 1831, Edward born 1829, Michael born 1834, and Patrick born 1823, daughters Honor born 1825, and Mary born 1827, from Ballykilcline, Kilglass parish, County Roscommon, emigrated from Liverpool on 18 October 1847 on the Creole, Captain Rattoone, to New York, arrived there 22 November 1847. [AH#22/339]

HANNA, ALEXANDER, born in Ireland during 1768, a runaway indentured servant in the Philadelphia Workhouse on 3 December 1784. [PaGaz#2846]

HANNA, ALEXANDER, born in Strabane, Ireland, 1767, emigrated from Sligo to America on the brig Rose, absconded from Thomas Mercer, Londonderry township, Chester County, on 27 April 1785. [PaJ#1797]

HANNA, JACOB, arrived in Canada on the Alexander on 3 June 1816, settled in Ketley, Ontario, on 30 June 1817. [PAO.MS154]

HANNAN, ANTHONY, born 1776, enlisted into the British Army in Tipperary 1804, discharged in Newfoundland 1818, settled in Dalhousie, Nova Scotia, 1820. [PRO.WO.25#548]

HARDY, THOMAS, arrived in Philadelphia from Londonderry on the brig Conyngham, master Robert Conyngham on 1 August 1789. [Pa.Pkt.11.8.1789]

HARNET, JAMES, from Ireland, settled near Philadelphia by 1775. [PaGaz#2404]

HARNET, THOMAS, born in Ireland during 1749, a runaway butcher and tanner servant, 1774. [Pa.Gaz.#2405]

HARNET, WILLIAM, from Ireland, settled near Philadelphia by 1775. [PaGaz#2404]

HARRIS, MICHAEL, an Anglican priest from Ireland, settled in Bathurst, Upper Canada, on 24 September 1816. [PAO.MS154]

HAYES, THOMAS, late of the Prince of York's Chasseurs, and his wife, settled in Beckwith, Ontario, on 21 October 1819. [PAO.MS154]

HENDERSON, JAMES, born in Ireland during 1743, absconded from John Craig, Warrington Township, Bucks County, Pennsylvania, May 1769. [PaGaz#2111]

HENRY, JAMES, born in Ireland during 1765, a weaver and indentured servant who absconded from William Ramsay in Northampton, Bucks County, Pennsylvania, 7 May 1785. [PaGaz#2868]

HEPBURN, SAMUEL, from Londonderry to Philadelphia on the Faithful Steward, shipwrecked off the Capes of Delaware in January 1786. [PEH#100]

HERROGAN, WILLIAM, born 1747, an Irish indentured servant who arrived in Philadelphia from Ireland on the Earl of Donegall, master Duncan Ferguson, in 1769, absconded from Benjamin Derow in Salem township, Pennsylvania, on 13 January 1772. [PaGaz.#2255]

HIGGINBOTTOM, ARTHUR, from Londonderry to Philadelphia on the Faithful Steward, shipwrecked off the Capes of Delaware in January 1786. [PEH#100]

HIGGINBOTHAM, JOHN, arrived in Canada on the Mary Ann on 8 August 1817, settled in Bathurst, Ontario, on 9 September 1817. [PAO.MS154]

HIGGINBOTHAM, ROBERT, arrived in Canada on the Mary Ann on 8 August 1817, settled in Bathurst, Ontario, on 9 September 1817. [PAO.MS154]

HILL, CHARLES, arrived in Newcastle, Delaware, from Londonderry on the brig Mary in November 1789. [Pa.Pkt, 5.12.1789]

HILL, WILLIAM, arrived in Newcastle, Delaware, from Londonderry on the brig Mary in November 1789. [Pa.Pkt, 5.12.1789]

HOARE, MICHAEL, born 1813, wife Mary born 1818, sons James born 1843, John born 1841, and Thomas born 1846, daughters Bridget born 1840 and and Mary born 1837, from Ballykilcline, Kilglass parish, County Roscommon, emigrated from Liverpool on 13 March 1848 on the Channing, Captain Huttleston, to New York, arrived there 17 April 1848. [AH#22/339]

HOGAN, MICHAEL, born 1780, enlisted into the British Army in Limerick 1804, discharged in St John 1818, settled in Dalhousie, Nova Scotia, 1820. [PRO.WO.25#548]

HOLBURN, THOMAS, born in Ireland during 1744, a woolcomber who absconded from David Beaty in Ulchland township, Chester County, Pennsylvania, on 4 June 1769. [PAGaz#2115]

HOLIDAY, THOMAS, born in Dungannon, County Tyrone, on 26 November 1774, died on 29 November 1829, buried in the Congregational Cemetery, Washington, D.C. [gravestone inscription]

HOLLAND, JAMES, late private of the Glengarry Fencibles, settled in Drummond, Ontario, on 16 July 1816. [PAO.MS154]

HOLLAND, JOHN, an Irish servant, absconded from John Crawford, constable in Gloucester, Pennsylvania, in March 1766. [PaJ#1215]

HORNER, ALEXANDER, born 1778, enlisted into the British Army in Templepatrick, County Antrim, 1804, discharged in St John 1818, settled in Dalhousie, Nova Scotia, 1820. [PRO.WO.25#548]

HOUGHY, THOMAS, born in Ireland during 1749, absconded from William Galbreath in York County, Pennsylvania, in August 1769. [PaGaz#2123]

HOWAY, JOHN, with his wife, 2 sons and 1 daughter, arrived in Canada on the Mary, on 20 July 1817, settled in Oxford, Ontario, on 9 September 1817. [PAO.MS154]

HOYLAND, ..., former Sergeant Major of the York Chasseurs, with his wife, settled in Bathurst, Ontario, on 1 October 1819. [PAO.MS154]

HUDSON, JAMES, born 1765, enlisted in the British Army in Tipperary 1804, discharged in St John 1818, settled in Dalhousie, Nova Scotia, 1820. [PRO.WO.25#548]

HUGHES, NICOLAS FORSTER, born in Ireland during 1739, absconded from James Old in Lancaster County, Pennsylvania, May 1769. [PaGaz#2111]

HUMPHRIES, JAMES, arrived in Philadelphia from Londonderry on the brig Conyngham, master Robert Conyngham on 1 August 1789. [Pa.Pkt.11.8.1789]

HUNT, JAMES P., born in Ireland during 1802, a clerk, arrived in Savannah late 1821 on the ship Georgia, Captain Varnum. [USNA]

HUSE, EDWARD, emigrated from Dublin on the snow Nancy, Captain Reilly, on 17 March 1787 bound for Baltimore, landed at Little River near Machias on 14 July 1787 and later at Newbury Port on 31 July 1787. [PaGaz#2985]

HUTCHISON, HUGH, born 1774, enlisted in the British Army in County Armagh 1805, discharged in St John, New Brunswick, 1818, settled in Dalhousie, Nova Scotia, 1820. [PRO.WO.25#548]

IRVINE, DAVID, with his wife, son and 3 daughters, arrived in Canada via USA, settled in Bathurst, Ontario, 31 December 1815. [PAO.MS154]

IRWIN, JAMES, late of the 97th Regiment, settled in Bathurst, Ontario, on 7 October 1819. [PAO.MS154]

JENKINSON, HENRY, born in Ireland during 1789, a labourer, with wife Ann born in Ireland during 1793, and 4 children, arrived in Oswegatchie, USA, on the boat Huron, master Graham, late 1821. [USNA]

JOHNSON, JOHN, late of the Glengarry Fencibles, settled in Bathurst, Ontario, on 23 July 1816. [PAO.MS154]

JOHNSON, ROBERT, settled in Melathon township, Home district, Ontario, on 5 September 1818. [PAO.MS154]

JOHNSTON, JAMES, born in Ireland during in 1743, absconded from Moore and Chestnut, brewers in Philadelphia, on 19 July 1769. [PaGaz#2117]

JONES, MARGARET, born in Ireland during in 1768, an indentured servant who absconded from John Hill in Middletown, Chester County, on 11 June 1786. [PaGaz#2926]

JONES, NELLY, born in Ireland during 1745, absconded from Hugh Jones, Lower Merion Township, Philadelphia, in May 1769. [PaGaz#2110]

JONES, THOMAS, born in Dublin, absconded from Joseph Anderson near the Blue Bell, Front Street, Philadelphia, in July 1769. [PaGaz#2117]

KAIN, JAMES, born in Ireland during 1767, immigrated into America on the Mary 1783, absconded from A. Lippincott, Springfield, Burlington County, in July 1784. [PaGaz#2824]

KANE, HENRY, arrived in Philadelphia on the Irish Volunteer, Captain Dillon, indentured servant of John Tyler a printer in Philadelphia, 1784. [PaMerc#7]

KARMAN, JAMES, born in Ireland during 1769, an indentured servant who absconded from James Duncan in Shippen Street, Philadelphia, on 18 September 1785. [PaGaz#2887]

KAVER, THOMAS, born in Ireland during 1801, a farmer, arrived in Philadelphia late 1821. [USNA]

KEARNEY, THOMAS, an Irish indentured servant who absconded from Jacob Walker in Radnor, Chester County, Pennsylvania, 10 April 1785. [PaGaz#2863]

KEASEY, PATRICK, born in Ireland during 1762, emigrated from Dublin to Philadelphia on the brig Liberty, shipwrecked on Hog Island, Virginia, resident in Belhaven, Virginia, then in Baltimore, jailed in Lancaster County, Lancaster, Pennsylvania, 6 June 1785. [PaJ#1817]

KEATING, WILLIAM, born in Mothel, Kilkenny, 1777, emigrated from Waterford to Halifax, Nova Scotia, on the Cumberland in June 1827, buried in Halifax on 23 July 1827. [Nova Scotia Historical Review#6/1.62]

KEATON, MICHAEL, born in Ireland during, a former officer of a British Light Horse unit, lately a stage player, sought for seizing a ship, 2 October 1784. [PaGaz#2837]

KEEGAN, JOHN, possibly from Dublin, formerly at Morris's Alley, Chestnut/Walnut Street, Philadelphia, dead by April 1769. [PaGaz#2110]

KEENAN, CHARLES, born in Ireland during 1764, an indentured servant who absconded from Richard Ford in Bark Creek, Pennsylvania, 30 November 1784. [PaGaz#2844]

KELLY, JOHN, born in Ireland during 1798, a carpenter, arrived in Philadelphia late 1821 on the brig Jane, Captain Richard. [USNA]

KELLY, ALEXANDER HAMILTON, a carpenter who immigrated from Ireland in 1783, absconded from John Boyle in Plumsted, Bucks County, Pennsylvania, 16 February 1785. [PaGaz#2857]

KELLY, JAMES, born 1803, wife Mary born 1808, sons Edward born 1830, James born 1832, and John born 1846, daughters Anne born 1836, Catherine born 1834, Eliza born 1838, Ellen born 1841, and Mary born 1828, from Ballykilcline, Kilglass parish, County Roscommon, emigrated from Liverpool on 13 March 1848 on the Channing, Captain Huttleston, to New York, arrived there 17 April 1848. [AH#22/339]

KELLY, MICHAEL, born in Dublin 1745, a convict indentured servant, absconded from his master James Hutcheson, Upper Deer Creek Hundred, Baltimore, Maryland, in October 1769. [PaGaz#2129]

KELLY, MICHAEL, born in Ireland during 1754, an indentured servant who absconded from James McCabe in Chester Church, Queens County, Maryland, in June 1784. [PaGaz#2824]

KELLY PATRICK, born 1808, (son-in-law of William Cline who sailed on the Channing, Captain Huttleston,), wife Eliza born 1812, sons Thomas born 1836 and William born 1840, daughters Anne born 1838, Bridget born 1847, and Maria born 1834, from Ballykilcline, Kilglass parish, County Roscommon, emigrated from Liverpool on 25 April 1848 on the Progress to New York. [AH#22/339]

KELLEY, THOMAS, born 1768, enlisted in the British Army in County Clare 1804, discharged in St John, 1818, settled in Dalhousie, Nova Scotia, 1820. [PRO.WO.25#548]

KELSO, HUGH, arrived in Newcastle, Delaware, from Londonderry on the brig Mary in November 1789. [Pa.Pkt, 5.12.1789]

KEMP, WILLIAM, County Cavan, settled at Rideau, Canada, 1820. [PAC:RG8.B22894/49]

KENNEDY, ANDREW, born in Ireland during 1801, a farmer, arrived in Philadelphia late 1821. [USNA]

KENNEDY, THOMAS, born in Ireland during in 1755, an indentured servant who absconded from Bucks County on 22 August 1785. [PaGaz#2882]

KENIFICK, DANIEL, born in Ireland during 1800, a farmer, arrived in New York on the ship Dublin Packet, Captain Newcomb. [USNA]

KENNY, NICHOLAS, born in Kilkenny, emigrated from Waterford to Halifax, Nova Scotia, on the Cumberland in June 1827, buried in Halifax 20 July 1827. [Nova Scotia Historical Review#6/1.62]

KERIGAN, NEAL, born in Ireland during in 1762, a shoemaker who immigrated on the brig Sisters, Captain Martin, in May 1784, an indentured servant who absconded from Paul Connor, Walnut Street, Pennsylvania, on 19 January 1785. [PaGaz#2851]

KERNAN, THOMAS, born in Dublin 1765, a runaway servant who was jailed in Reading, Berks County, on 18 May 1787. [PaGaz#2977]

KERNEY, WILLIAM, born in Ireland during 1801, a farmer, arrived in New York late 1821 on the ship Dublin Packet, Captain Newcomb. [USNA]

KERRINGTON, THOMAS, late of the Glengarry Fencibles, settled in Bathurst, Ontario, on 23 July 1816. [PAO.MS154]

KERWIN, THOMAS, born in County Waterford, 1787, a tailor, emigrated from Waterford to Halifax, Nova Scotia, on the Cumberland in June 1827, buried in Halifax 12.7.1827. [Nova Scotia Historical Review#6/1.62]

KEVIL, PATRICK, a laborer, an indentured servant, who immigrated from Ireland on the Favourite, master Robert Alcorn, to Philadelphia in July 1784. [PaGaz#2832]

KEYS, JAMES, from Newtonbarry, Ireland, settled at Rideau, Canada, 1820. [PAC:RG8.B22894/49]

KINCADE, MARGARET, from Londonderry to Philadelphia on the Faithful Steward, shipwrecked off the Capes of Delaware in January 1786. [PEH#100]

KIRBY, JOHN, born in Ireland during, a butcher, who immigrated from Ireland in May 1784, an indentured servant, who absconded from Henry Miller in Philadelphia on 31 October 1784. [PaGaz#2839]

KIRKPATRICK, SAMUEL, Londonderry, admitted as a member of the Scots Charitable Society of Boston 1694. [NEHGS/SCSpp]

KIRKWOOD, THOMAS, arrived in Philadelphia from Londonderry on the brig Conyngham, master Robert Conyngham on 1 August 1789. [Pa.Pkt.11.8.1789]

KNOWLER, PATRICK, born in Ireland during 1767, immigrated into America on the Mary 1783, an indentured servant who absconded from A. Lippincott in Springfield, Burlington County, in July 1784. [PaGaz#2824]

LAIRD, JOHN, born in Ireland during 1761, an indentured servant who absconded from Henry Dills at Mount Bethel, Northampton County, Pennsylvania, in March 1786. [PaGaz#2914]

LAND, ELIZABETH, born in 1727, a servant who absconded from the sloop Jean, Captain Cook, in June 1765, which had recently arrived from Cork. [PaJ#1175]

LANGAN, PATRICK, a joiner, an indentured servant, who immigrated from Ireland on the Favourite, master Robert Alcorn, to Philadelphia in July 1784. [PaGaz#2832]

LATIMER, HARRY, late Sergeant of the Royal Artillery, settled in Burgess, Ontario, on 26 October 1819. [PAO.MS154]

LAURENCE, ROBERT, from Londonderry to Philadelphia on the Faithful Steward, shipwrecked off the Capes of Delaware in January 1786. [PEH#100]

LAUGHLIN, THOMAS, born in Ireland during 1755, escaped from the Sheriff of Franklin County, Pennsylvania, in November 1785. [PaGaz#2895]

LEACH, RICHARD, arrived in Canada on the brig Charles Millar on 19 September 1815, settled in Drummond, Ontario, on 16 November 1815. [PAO.MS154]

LEACY, CADNEY, an Irish servant, absconded from Richard Lemon, Newark, Newcastle County, in January 1770. [PaJ#1416]

LEAN, JOSEPH, late private of the Glengarry Regiment, settled in Drummond, Ontario, on 18 July 1816. [PAO.MS154]

LEE, RICHARD, an Irish indentured servant who absconded from his master R. Hutchison in Charleston, South Carolina, in May 1734. [SCGaz#17]

LEONARD, MATTHEW, Irish, in Chester gaol, Pennsylvania, on 20 May 1765. [PaJ#1172]

LEARY, DANIEL, born in Ireland during 1749, absconded from John Phipps, Chester County, Pennsylvania, on 12 August 1769. [PaGaz#2120]

LEE, JAMES, from Londonderry to Philadelphia on the Faithful Steward, shipwrecked off the Capes of Delaware in January 1786. [PEH#100]

LEE, MARY, from Londonderry to Philadelphia on the Faithful Steward, shipwrecked off the Capes of Delaware in January 1786. [PEH#100]

LESTER, GEORGE, with his wife, 3 sons and 4 daughters, settled in Bathurst, Ontario, on 1 November 1816. [PAO.MS154]

LEWIS, Mrs, born in Ireland during 1799, and child, arrived in Savannah late 1821 on the ship Georgia Captain Varnum. [USNA]

LOGAN, HENRY, born in Ireland during 1763, an indentured servant, absconded from William Starrett in East Nantmill township, Chester County, Pennsylvania, on 28 May 1784. [PaGaz#2822]

LOGAN, JAMES, born 1753 in the north of Ireland, absconded from Edward Milne in Philadelphia on 3 August 1769. [PaGaz#2118]

LOGAN, MARY, born in Ireland during 1791, with 2 children, arrived in New York late 1821. [USNA]

LONERGAN, MICHAEL, born 1776, enlisted in the British Army in Cork 1805, discharged in St John, 1818, settled in Dalhousie, Nova Scotia, 1820. [PRO.WO.25#548]

LONERGAN, WILLIAM, sr., born 1773, enlisted in the British Army in Cork 1805, discharged in St John, 1818, settled in Dalhousie, Nova Scotia, 1820. [PRO.WO.25#548]

LONERGAN, WILLIAM, born 1779, enlisted in the British Army in Cashel, Tipperary, 1804, discharged in Fredericton, New Brunswick, 1818, settled in Dalhousie, Nova Scotia, 1820. [PRO.WO.25#548]

LONG, JAMES, born 1776, enlisted in the British Army in Cashel, Tipperary, 1804, discharged in Newfoundland, 1818, settled in Dalhousie, Nova Scotia, 1820. [PRO.WO.25#548]

LOOBY, PATRICK, an Irish indentured servant who absconded from James Brown and Richard Strode in West Bradford, Chester County, Pennsylvania, on 12 June 1786. [PaGaz#2923]

LOWREY, JOHN, emigrated from Waterford to Halifax, Nova Scotia, on the Cumberland in June 1827. [Nova Scotia Hist. Review#6/1.61]

LYONS, WILLIAM, a fuller and dyer, an indentured servant who absconded from the brigantine Nancy, master Daniel Dingee, which arrived in Philadelphia from Cork on 9 June 1769. [PaGaz#2112/2114]

MCALIEFF, HENRY, born in Ireland during 1730, a shoemaker who absconded from Cornelius Bryan, Raccoon Creek, Greenwich township, Gloucester County, Pennsylvania, in June 1765. [PaJ#1175]

MCALLESTER, DANIEL, who immigrated from Ireland on the Irish Volunteer, escaped from jail in Newtown, Pennsylvania, on 10 October 1784. [PaGaz#2838]

MCANITINIE, DANIEL, born 1750 in Ireland, absconded from Michael Finley and John Crawford in Carrol's Tract, York County, Pennsylvania, on 15 December 1771. [PaGaz#2245]

MCAULAY, ARTHUR, arrived in Canada on the Fame on 28 May 1815, settled in Beckwith, Ontario, on 30 November 1815. [PAO.MS154]

MCAVOY, THOMAS, born 1795 in Clary, Queens County, Ireland, died in Washington County, Maryland, on 29 March 1850. [Methodist Cemetery, Hancock, Maryland]

MCCABE, JOHN, alias KNOWLES, born in Ireland during 1760, immigrated in May 1784 on the Three Friends, Captain Watson, absconded from the ship in Philadelphia, captured and jailed in Easton, Northampton County, on 31 July 1784. [PaGaz#2827]

MACCALLISTER, JOHN, from Londonderry to Philadelphia on the Faithful Steward, shipwrecked off the Capes of Delaware in January 1786. [PEH#100]

MACARTNEY, FANNY, daughter of J. Macartney a banker in Carlow, married C. Ranaldson Fickson, second son of David R. Dickson of Blairhall, Perthshire, in Hamilton, Upper Canada, on 7 January 1843. [AJ#4965]

MCCARTY, WILLIAM, born in Ireland during 1765, an indentured servant who absconded from Thomas Bull in Chester County on 14 November 1785. [PaGaz#2895]

MCCLEAN, HUGH, from Londonderry to Philadelphia on the Faithful Steward, shipwrecked off the Capes of Delaware in January 1786. [PEH#100]

MCCIB, JAMES, born 1757, a Scotch-Irish servant who absconded from John Zimberman in Providence, Montgomery County, on 7 April 1787. [PaGaz#2971]

MCCLINTOCK, WILLIAM, from Londonderry to Philadelphia on the Faithful Steward, shipwrecked off the Capes of Delaware in January 1786. [PEH#100]

MCCONNELL, WILLIAM, born in Ireland during 1767, an indentured servant who absconded from Barzilia Ridgway in Springfield, Burlington County, New Jersey, in December 1784. [PaGaz#2846]

MCCONNELLY, BERNARD, born 1777, enlisted in the British Army in Louth, 1805, discharged in St John, New Brunswick, 1818, settled in Dalhousie, Nova Scotia, 1820. [PRO.WO.25#548]

MCCOOK, JOHN, arrived from Ireland in December 1774, an indentured servant who absconded from James Molesworth, at the widow Yarnell's, Chestnut Street, Philadelphia, 1775. [PaGaz#2407]

MCCORMICK, CATHERINE, born 1792, sons Patrick born 1825 and Peter born 1832, daughters Anne born 1838 and Ellen born 1817, from Ballykilcline, Kilglass parish, County Roscommon, emigrated from Liverpool on 26 September 1847 on the Metoka to New York, arrived there 30 October 1847. [AH#22/339]

MCCORMICK, EDWARD, born 1807, wife Margaret born 1815, sons Edward born 1843, James born 1846, and Thomas born 1839, with Anne born 1833, Catherine born 1841, and Mary born 1829 born 1832, from Ballykilcline, Kilglass parish, County Roscommon, emigrated from Liverpool on 26 September 1847 on the Metoka to New York, arrived there 30 October 1847. [AH#22/339]

MCCORMICK, JAMES, born 1744 in Ireland, absconded from Michael Finley and John Crawford in Carrol's Tract, York County, Pennsylvania, on 15 December 1771. [PaGaz#2245]

MCCORMICK, MARY, born 1821, sister Anne born 1827, sister Bridget born 1823, brother Michael born 1828, sister Honor born 1830, sister Margaret born 1828, and sister Sally born 1831, from Ballykilcline, Kilglass parish, County Roscommon, emigrated from Liverpool on 26 September 1847 on the Metoka to New York, arrived there 30 October 1847. [AH#22/339]

MCCORMICK, MICHAEL, born 1828, sister Honor born 1830, sister Margaret born 1828, and sister Sally born 1831, from Ballykilcline, Kilglass parish, County Roscommon, emigrated from Liverpool on 18 October 1847 on the Creole, Captain Rattoone, to New York, arrived there 22 November 1847. [AH#22/339]

MCCORMICK, PATRICK, born 1816, wife Catherine born 1819, son Michael born 1843, son Patrick born 1841, daughter Anne born 1839, with Mary born 1827 sister of Patrick, from Ballykilcline, Kilglass parish, County Roscommon, emigrated from Liverpool on 13 March 1848 on the Channing, Captain Huttleston, to New York, arrived there 17 April 1848. [AH#22/339]

MCCORMACK, WILLIAM, born in County Tyrone, a tailor and indentured servant who absconded from Elijah Cozens in Greenwich, Gloucester County, West New Jersey, on 2 February 1786. [PaGaz#2917]

MCCORRY, EDWIN, born 1800 in Ireland, a farmer, arrived in New York late 1821 on the ship Dublin Packet, Captain Newcomb. [USNA]

MCCOUGLIN, SAMUEL, born in Ireland during 1797, a carpenter, arrived in Philadelphia late 1821. [USNA]

MCCREASY, HUGH, born in Ireland during 1781, a weaver, with Susanna born in Ireland during 1791, and children, arrived in Waldboro, USA, late 1821 on the ship Lydia, Captain Adams. [USNA]

MCCULLOUGH, BARNABAS, born in Ireland during 1746, escaped from the Sheriff of Bucks County, Pennsylvania, in December 1771. [PaGaz#2245]

MCCUE, FREDERICK, born 1741 in Ireland, absconded from Charles Harah, Little Britain township, Lancaster County, Pennsylvania, on 10 December 1771. [PaGaz#2245]

MCCUE, JAMES, born in Ireland during ca1756, a shoemaker and runaway from John Stevenson in New York 1786. [Pa.J#2129]

MCCULOUGH, SAMUEL, son of John McCulough late of Mamacullen, County Armagh, later resident in Woodbridge, New Jersey, sought in Pennsylvania on 30 May 1765. [PaJ#1172]

MCDANIEL, MICHAEL, born in Ireland during ca.1751, a runaway servant from Cecil County, 1 December 1774. [Pa.Gaz.#2405]

MCDERMOTT, HUGH, born 1797, wife Eliza born 1799, sons Bernard born 1819, Hugh born 1835, James born 1821, John born 1823, and William born 1829, daughters Anne born 1822, Bessy born 1827, Ellen born 1824, Rosanna born 1833, and Susan born 1825, from Ballykilcline, Kilglass parish, County Roscommon, emigrated from Liverpool on 19 September 1847 on the Roscius, Captain Eldridge, to New York, arrived there 21 October 1847. [AH#22/343]

MCDERMOTT, MARY, born 1803, sons John born 1834 and Thomas born 1832, daughters Ellen born 1827, Mary born 1830, and Bridget born 1836, from Ballykilcline, Kilglass parish, County Roscommon, emigrated from Liverpool on 30 September 1847 on the Metoka, Captain McGuire, to New York, arrived there 30 October 1847. [AH#22/343]

MCDERMOTT, MICHAEL, born 1803, wife Ellen born 1807, son Michael born 1831, daughters Anne born 1839, Betty born 1834, Ellen born 1837, and Mary born 1830, from Ballykilcline, Kilglass parish, County Roscommon, emigrated from Liverpool on 30 September 1847 on the Metoka, Captain McGuire,to New York, arrived there 30 October 1847. [AH#22/343]

MCDONNELL, ANDREW, born 1830, sister Anne born 1826, sister Ellen born 1832, from Ballykilcline, Kilglass parish, County Roscommon, emigrated from Liverpool on 13 March 1848 on the Channing, Captain Huttleston, to New York, arrived there 17 April 1848. [AH#22/343]

MCDONALL, ALEXANDER, weaver, indented in Dublin on 9 March 1727 with Samuel Moor, arrived in New York on the George 17 June 1728, settled in Middletown, New Jersey.

MCDONALL, JOHN, County Antrim, pro. Anne Arundel County, Maryland, 1.12.1772. [will Liber 39, fo.251]

MCDONNELL, MICHAEL, born 1798, son Michael born 1827, daughters Catherine born 1824 and Mary born 1830, from Ballykilcline, Kilglass parish, County Roscommon, emigrated from Liverpool on 13 March 1848 on the Channing, Captain Huttleston, to New York, arrived there 17 April 1848. [AH#22/343]

MCDONNELL, PATRICK, born 1823, from Ballykilcline, Kilglass parish, County Roscommon, emigrated from Liverpool on 26 September 1847 on the Metoka to New York, arrived there 30 October 1847. [AH22/343]

MCDONNELL, PATRICK, born 1775 in the parish of Templemuhal, County Longford, died 8 September 1823. [Hancock cemetery, Maryland, g/s]

MCDONNEL, THOMAS, emigrated from Dublin on the snow Nancy, Captain Reilly, on 17 March 1787 bound for Baltimore, landed at Little River near Machias on 14 July 1787 and later at Newbury Port on 31 July 1787. [PaGaz#2985]

MCDOUGLE, Dr .., from Londonderry to Philadelphia on the Faithful Steward, shipwrecked off the Capes of Delaware in January 1786. [PEH#100]

MCGANN, JOHN, born 1824, brothers Atty born 1829, Luke born 1828, sisters Anne born 1822, and Mary born 1823, with John McGann born 1847, from Ballykilcline, Kilglass parish, County Roscommon, emigrated from Liverpool on 13 March 1848 on the Channing, Captain Huttleston, to New York, arrived there 17 April 1848. [AH22/343]

MCGANN, MARY, born 1808, sons James born 1830, John born 1843, Thomas born 1840, and daughters Anne born 1847, Bridget born 1838, and Eliza born 1834, from Ballykilcline, Kilglass parish, County Roscommon, emigrated from Liverpool on 13 March 1848 on the Channing, Captain Huttleston, to New York, arrived there 17 April 1848. [AH22/343]

MCGRAW, THOMAS, born in Ireland during, a former marine, absconded from John Vansart, Kent County, Maryland, on 10 July 1769. [PaGaz#2117]

MCFADDIN, STREINGER, with wife, 5 sons and 6 daughters, arrived in Canada on the Alexander on 1 April 1817, settled in Edwardsburgh, Ontario, on 27 June 1817. [PAO.MS154]

MCFARLANE, JAMES, arrived in Newcastle, Delaware, from Londonderry on the brig Mary in November 1789. [Pa.Pkt, 5.12.1789]

MCGILL, JAMES, born 1784, enlisted in the British Army in Cavan, 1805, discharged 1818, settled in Dalhousie, Nova Scotia, 1820. [PRO.WO.25#548]

MCGILL, ROBERT, born 1795, enlisted in the British Army in County Tyrone, 1813, discharged in St John 1818, settled in Dalhousie, Nova Scotia, 1820. [PRO.WO.25#548]

MCGINLY, HUGH, from Lefford parish, County Donegal, settled in Philadelphia 1770. [PaGaz#2147]

MCGINLAY, NEAL, from Lefford parish, County Donegal, settled in America before 1770. [PaGaz#2147]

MCGINNIS, MARGARET, from Londonderry to Philadelphia on the Faithful Steward, shipwrecked off the Capes of Delaware in January 1786. [PEH#100]

MCGOWAN, PATRICK, born in Ireland during 1798, a laborer, arrived in Newberryport, USA, late 1821. [USNA]

MCGOWAN, THOMAS, born 1778, enlisted in the British Army in County Armagh, 1805, discharged in St John 1818, settled in Dalhousie, Nova Scotia, 1820. [PRO.WO.25#548]

MAGUIRE, FRANCIS, born in Ireland during 1799, a farmer, arrived in New York late 1821. [USNA]

MCGUIRE, THOMAS, Irish servant, absconded from Richard Graves, Warton Creek, Kent County, Maryland, on 10 April 1785. [PaJ#1795]

MCGUIRK, ANN, born in Ireland during 1802, arrived in Waldboro, USA, late 1821 on the ship Lydia, Captain Adams. [USNA]

MCILKENNY, JOHN, from Londonderry to Philadelphia on the Faithful Steward, shipwrecked off the Capes of Delaware in January 1786. [PEH#100]

MCINTIRE, JAMES, sr., from Londonderry to Philadelphia on the Faithful Steward, shipwrecked off the Capes of Delaware in January 1786. [PEH#100]

MCINTIRE, JAMES, jr., from Londonderry to Philadelphia on the Faithful Steward, shipwrecked off the Capes of Delaware in January 1786. [PEH#100]

MCINTIRE, REBECCA, from Londonderry to Philadelphia on the Faithful Steward, shipwrecked off the Capes of Delaware in January 1786. [PEH#100]

MCKAY, Reverend DAVID, emigrated from Belfast to America on the Prince George, master R. Beatty, arrived on 7 December 1768, later pastor of Williamsburg, South Carolina. [GaGaz#271]

MCKAY, JAMES, a mariner from Londonderry, died in Antigua, pro.1693 PCC

MCKAEHILL, EDWARD, born in Ireland during 1768, immigrated from Ireland to Philadelphia on the Volunteer in 1783, an indentured servant who absconded from Andrew Ledlie in Easton, Pennsylvania(?), on 4 August 1784. [PaGaz#2828]

MCKESSON, ALEXANDER, from Ireland 1731, settled in Fag's Manor, Chester County, Pennsylvania, father of John born on 20 February 1734. [ANY.I.17]

MCKEY, JOHN, sr., with his wife, 2 sons and 2 daughters, arrived in Canada via USA, settled in Bathurst, Ontario, on 31 December 1815. [PAO.MS154]

MCKEY, JOHN, jr., arrived in Canada via USA, settled in Bathurst, Ontario, on 9 December 1815. [PAO.MS154]

MCKINNEY, MARTIN, born 1746 in Ireland, absconded from Robert McConnel in Cumberland County, Letterkenny township, Pennsylvania, on 23 July 1771. [PaGaz#2245]

MCKINNON, NEIL, from Londonderry to Philadelphia on the Faithful Steward, shipwrecked off the Capes of Delaware in January 1786. [PEH#100]

MACHALEY, PATRICK, Ireland, absconded from Alexander Snodgrass, Little Britain township, Lancaster County, Pennsylvania, on 28 December 1771. [PaGaz#2246]

MCKINNY, M., born in Ireland during 1791, with 3 children, arrived in Newberryport, USA, late 1821. [USNA]

MCLAUGHLIN, MARGARET, born in Ireland during 1793, with 2 children, arrived in Waldboro, USA, late 1821 on the ship Lydia, Captain Adams. [USNA]

MCLEAN, JAMES, Sergeant of the Glengarry Fencibles, settled in Wolford, Ontario, on 25 October 1819. [PAO.MS154]

MCMAHON, FRANCIS, born 1791, enlisted in the British Army in Dublin, 1811, discharged from the 8th Regiment in St John's, Newfoundland, 1818, settled in Dalhousie, Nova Scotia, 1820. [PRO.WO.25#548]

MCMAHON, HUGH, private of the Glengarry Fencibles, settled in Wolford, Ontario, on 16 July 1816. [PAO.MS154]

MCMANUS, MATTHEW, from Londonderry to Philadelphia on the Faithful Steward, shipwrecked off the Capes of Delaware in January 1786. [PEH#100]

MCMANUS, THOMAS, born 1819, with brother James born 1828, from Ballykilcline, Kilglass parish, County Roscommon, emigrated from Liverpool on 13 March 1848 on the Channing, Captain Huttleston, to New York, arrived there 17 April 1848. [AH22/344]

MCMANUS, THOMAS, born 1824, with brothers Andrew born 1827, Patrick born 1825, and Mary born 1830, from Ballykilcline, Kilglass parish, County Roscommon, emigrated from Liverpool on 13 March 1848 on the Channing, Captain Huttleston, to New York, arrived there 17 April 1848. [AH22/344]

MCMULLEN, JOHN, from Londonderry to Philadelphia on the Faithful Steward, shipwrecked off the Capes of Delaware in January 1786. [PEH#100]

MCMULLEN, PATRICK, emigrated from Dublin on the snow Nancy, Captain Reilly, on 17 March 1787 bound for Baltimore, landed at Little River near Machias on 14 July 1787 and later at Newbury Port on31 July 1787. [PaGaz#2985]

MCNAB, JOHN, from Londonderry to Philadelphia on the Faithful Steward, shipwrecked off the Capes of Delaware in January 1786. [PEH#100]

MACNAMEE, PATRICK, with his wife and daughter, settled in Burgess, Ontario, 1.11.1816. [PAO.MS154]

MCNEELY, HUGH, arrived in Newcastle, Delaware, from Londonderry on the brig Mary 11.1789. [Pa.Pkt, 5.12.1789]

MCNELIS, JOHN, born in Ireland during 1865, an indentured servant who absconded from Richard Jones in East Bradford, Chester County, Pennsylvania, on 8 September 1784. [PaGaz#2832]

MCNELTY, PATRICK, County Mayo, declared his intent to become a US citizen in Craven County, North Carolina, on 13 August 1834. [Craven County Court Records]

MCNICE, JAMES, late Sergeant of the Glengarry Fencibles, settled in Bastard, Ontario, 20 October 1819. [PAO.MS154]

MCNINCH, JOHN, born in Ireland during 1749, a house carpenter who absconded from William Wallace, Hopewell township. York County, Pennsylvania , on 12 June 1769. [PAGaz#2116]

MCOWEN, OWEN, born in Ireland during 1757, an indentured servant who absconded from Henry Howard near Baltimore, Maryland, on 13 July 1784. [PaGaz#2836]

MCPEAK, JOHN, settled in Brock township, Newcastle district, Ontario, on 11 October 1817. [PAO.MS154]

MCPHADDIN, MICHAEL, born in Ireland during 1759, an indentured servant who absconded from Bucks County, on 22 August 1785. [PaGaz#2882]

MCWILLIAMS, CHARLES, from Londonderry to Philadelphia on the Faithful Steward, shipwrecked off the Capes of Delaware in January 1786. [PEH#100]

MADDEN, MARY, born 1802, son Thomas born 1835, and daughter Catherine born 1832, from Ballykilcline, Kilglass parish, County Roscommon, emigrated from Liverpool on 13 March 1848 on the Channing, Captain Huttleston, to New York, arrived there 17 April 1848. [AH22/344]

MAGAN, JOHN, born 1813, brother Patrick born 1825, sisters Anne born 1819, Ellen born 1821, and Catherine born 1823, from Ballykilcline, Kilglass parish, County Roscommon, emigrated from Liverpool on 18 October 1847 on the Creole, Captain Rattoone, to New York, arrived there 22 November 1847. [AH22/344]

MAGEE, CHARLES, born in Ireland during, a butcher and indentured servant, who absconded from Evan Evans, Uwchland, Chester County, Pennsylvania, 17 April 1785. [PaGaz#2865]

MAGUIRE, JOHN, born 1817, wife Mary born 1817, son Patrick born 1842, and daughter Mary born 1844, from Ballykilcline, Kilglass parish, County Roscommon, emigrated from Liverpool on 18 October 1847 on the Creole, Captain Rattoone, to New York, arrived there 22 November 1847. [AH22/344]

MAHER, JOHN, a gentleman's servant and indentured servant who absconded from the brigantine Nancy, master Daniel Dingee, which arrived in Philadelphia from Cork on 9 June 1769. [PaGaz#2112/2114]

MAHONEY, JOHN, alias JOHN NOONIN, born in Ireland during 1768, an indentured servant who absconded from Henry Howard near Baltimore, Maryland, on 3 July 1784. [PaGaz#2836]

MALLOY, MICHAEL, born in Ireland during 1748, an indentured servant who absconded from the brig Hawk, master Bennet Matthews, when it arrived at Philadelphia from Waterford on 18 June 1769. [PaGaz#2114]

MALONE, EDWARD, born in Ireland during 1801, a tailor, arrived in Philadelphia late 1821. [USNA]

MALONE, CHARLES, Ireland, indented for 4 years service in Jamaica in London on 28 April 1685. [CLRO/AIA#14/228]

MARCH, ANTHONY, born in Ireland during 1802, a farmer, arrived in Waldboro, USA, late 1821 on the ship Lydia, Captain Adams. [USNA]

MARCHBANK, I., born in Ireland during 1827, settled in Cherokee County, Georgia, by 1850. [1850 Census]

MARSHALL, JAMES, from Londonderry to Philadelphia on the Faithful Steward, shipwrecked off the Capes of Delaware in January 1786. [PEH#100]

MATHESON, ALEXANDER, late Quarter Master Sergeant of the Glengarry Fencibles, settled in Drummond, Ontario, on 23 July 1816. [PAO.MS154]

MAUDE, THOMAS, arrived in Canada on the brig John on 3 September 1815, settled in Beckwith, Ontario, on 9 December 1815. [PAO.MS154]

MEANEY, JOHN, born in 1787 in Brownstown, Kilkenny, emigrated from Waterford to Halifax, Nova Scotia, on the Cumberland, arrived 6.1827, buried on 12 July 1827.[Nova Scotia Hist. Review#6/1.61]

MILLER, HUGH, born in Ireland during 1802, a farmer, arrived in Waldboro, USA, late 1821 on the ship Lydia, Captain Adams. [USNA]

MILLOWNEY, MAURICE, late of the Glengarry Fencibles, settled Bathurst, Ontario, on 23 July 1816. [PAO.MS154]

MITCHELL, DANIEL, late private of the 88th Regiment, settled in Drummond, Ontario, on 14 July 1816. [PAO.MS154]

MITCHELL, ROBERT, a weaver, a runaway from the Faithful Steward of Londonderry in Philadelphia 31 August 1784. [PaGaz#2830]

MONTGOMERY, CHARLES, born in Ireland during in 1798, a farmer, arrived in Philadelphia late 1821 on the brig Rising Sun, Captain Prince. [USNA]

MONTGOMERY, JOHN, of Ballevely, County Antrim, a Cornet in Charles II Lifeguards in Scotland, standard bearer at the Battle of Dunbar 1650, later fought at Warrington and at Worcester 1651, captured there and transported to Virginia. Petitioned the Privy Council February 1661. [Calendar of State Papers, Ireland, 1661/242]

MONTGOMERY, JOSEPH, born in Ireland during 1806, a farmer, arrived in Philadelphia late 1821 on the brig Rising Sun Captain Prince. [USNA]

MONTGOMERY, MARGARET, born in Ireland during in 1767, an indentured servant who absconded from Francis Johnston, Water Street, Philadelphia, on 6 July 1785. [PaGaz#2878]

MOODY, JOHN, born in Ireland during 1765, a runaway indentured servant jailed in Chester on 13 October 1785. [PaGaz#2892]

MOORE, ALEXANDER, from Londonderry to Philadelphia on the Faithful Steward, shipwrecked off the Capes of Delaware in January 1786. [PEH#100]

MOORE, THOMAS, from Londonderry to Philadelphia on the Faithful Steward, shipwrecked off the Capes of Delaware in January 1786. [PEH#100]

MOORE, WALSINGHAM, with his wife, 3 sons and 2 daughters, arrived in Canada on the Mary Ann on 8 August 1817, settled in Yonge, Ontario, on 12 September 1817. [PAO.MS154]

MOORE, WILLIAM, and his daughter, arrived in Canada on the Mary Ann on 8 August 1817, settled in Yonge, Ontario, on 12 September 1817. [PAO.MS154]

MORAN, JOHN, born 1791, wife Winifred born 1803, sons Francis born 1840 and John born 1832, and daughter Catherine born 1837, from Ballykilcline, Kilglass parish, County Roscommon, emigrated from Liverpool on 26 September 1847 on the Metoka to New York, arrived there 30 October 1847. [AH22/344]

MORGAN, WILLIAM, from Barris Cane, Tipperary, settled at Rideau, Canada, in 1820. [PAC: RG8.B22894/49]

MOORE, RICHARD, arrived in Philadelphia from Londonderry on the brig Conyngham, master Robert Conyngham on 1 August 1789. [Pa.Pkt.11.8.1789]

MOORE, ROBERT, late Sergeant of the 104th Regiment, settled in Bathurst, Ontario, on 17 December 1819. [PAO.MS154]

MOORE, SAMUEL, from Londonderry to Philadelphia on the Faithful Steward, shipwrecked off the Capes of Delaware in January 1786. [PEH#100]

MOOREHOUSE, JOHN, settled in Beckwith, Ontario, on 28 December 1819. [PAO.MS154]

MORNER, THOMAS, arrived in Canada on the brig John on 3 September 1815, settled in Drummond, Ontario, on 9 December 1815. [PAO.MS154]

MORRIS, JOHN, arrived in Canada on the brig John on 3 September 1815, settled in Beckwith, Ontario, on 9 December 1815. [PAO.MS154]

MORRIS, SAMUEL, arrived in Canada on the Mary Ann, on 8 August 1817, settled in Yonge, Ontario, on 13 September 1817. [PAO.MS154]

MORRIS, THOMAS, with his wife, 2 sons and 4 daughters, arrived in Canada on the Mary Ann, on 8 August 1817, settled in Yonge, Ontario, on 13 September 1817. [PAO.MS154]

MOULTON, WILLIAM, with his wife, son and 2 daughters, arrived in Canada on the Mary Ann on 8 August 1817, settled in Yonge, Ontario, on 9 September 1817. [PAO.MS154]

MULANIE, RICHARD, born in Ireland during 1724, absconded from Joshua Owings, Baltimore County, Maryland, on 6 February 1769. [PaGaz#2103]

MULLEN, DANIEL, born in Ireland during 1750, absconded from Arthur Broades, Fuller, Upper Dublin, Philadelphia County, on 26 December 1765. [PaJ#1205]

MULLEN, JAMES, born in Ireland during 1798, a shoemaker, arrived in Waldboro, USA, late 1821 on the ship Lydia, Captain Adams. [USNA]

MULLERA, ANNE, born 1823, with Patrick Mullera born 1819, from Ballykilcline, Kilglass parish, County Roscommon, emigrated from Liverpool on 13 March 1848 on the Channing, Captain Huttleston, to New York, arrived there 17 April 1848. [AH22/344]

MULLERA, CATHERINE, born 1817, from Ballykilcline, Kilglass parish, County Roscommon, emigrated from Liverpool on 21 October 1847 on the Roscius, Captain Eldridge, to New York, arrived there 21 October 1847. [AH22/344]

MULLERA, JAMES, born 1797, wife Bridget born 1797, son Denis born 1835, and daughters Anne born 1838 and Bridget born 1837, from Ballykilcline, Kilglass parish, County Roscommon, emigrated from Liverpool on 18 October 1847 on the Creole, Captain Rattoone, to New York, arrived there 22 November 1847. [AH22/344]

MULLERA, JAMES, born 1825, and brother Thomas born 1827, from Ballykilcline, Kilglass parish, County Roscommon, emigrated from Liverpool on 26 September 1847 on the Metoka to New York, arrived there 30 October 1847. [AH22/344]

MULLERA, JOHN, born 1813, wife Sarah born 1818, sons Francis born 1842, James born 1844, John born 1840, Patrick born 1836, and Thomas born 1838, with John's brother Patrick born 1823, from Ballykilcline, Kilglass parish, County Roscommon, emigrated from Liverpool on 13 April 1848 on the Channing, Captain Huttleston, to New York, arrived there 17 April 1848 [AH22/345]

MULLERA, THOMAS, born 1812, wife Mary born 1818, son Thomas born 1832, daughter Anne born 1846, with Thomas's mother Bridget born 1793, from Ballykilcline, Kilglass parish, County Roscommon, emigrated from Liverpool on 13 April 1848 on the Channing, Captain Huttleston, to New York, arrived there 17 April 1848 [AH22/345]

MULLINS, JOHN, born in Ireland during 1804, a farmer, arrived in New York late 1821 on the ship Dublin Packet, Captain Newcomb. [USNA]

MULVANEY, JOHN, born in Ireland during 1761, a weaver and indentured servant who absconded from William Long at the Head of Falling Spring, Franklin County, Pennsylvania, on 30 July 1786. [PaGaz#2926]

MUNROE, GEORGE, from Londonderry to Philadelphia on the Faithful Steward, shipwrecked off the Capes of Delaware in January 1786. [PEH#100]

MURPHY, CORNELIUS, born in 1792, enlisted in the British Army in Kilbrogan, Cork, during 1813, discharged in Fredericton, New Brunswick, in 1818, settled in Dalhousie, Nova Scotia, in 1820. [PRO.WO.25#548]

MURPHY, DANIEL, an Irish servant, absconded from David Llewellyin, Pencader Hundred, Newcastle County, in May 1769. [PaGaz#2110]

MURPHY, GARRET, born in Ireland during 1745, absconded from Samuel Henry in Philadelphia on 13 August 1769. [PaGaz#2122]

MURPHY, JAMES, born in Ireland during 1800, an accountant, arrived in Philadelphia late 1821 on the brig Jane, Captain Richard. [USNA]

MURPHY, JOHN, born in Ireland during 1802, a clerk, arrived in New York late 1821 on the ship Dublin Packet, Captain Newcomb. [USNA]

MURPHY, MATHEW, born in Ireland, wanted for burglary in Philadelphia on 27 July 1769. [PaGaz#2117]

MURPHY, MOSES, arrived in Canada on the Mary and Betty on 19 September 1816, settled in Drummond, Ontario, on 28 January 1817. [PAO.MS154]

MURPHY, PETER, emigrated from Dublin on the snow Nancy, Captain Reilly, on 17 March 1787 bound for Baltimore, landed at Little River near Machias on 14 July 1787 and later at Newbury Port on 31 July 1787. [PaGaz#2985]

MURPHY, TIMOTHY, emigrated from Dublin on the snow Nancy, Captain Reilly, on 17 March 1787 bound for Baltimore, landed at Little River near Machias on 14 July 1787 and later at Newbury Port on 31 July 1787. [PaGaz#2985]

MURPHY, WILLIAM, late Sergeant of the Canadian Fencibles, settled in Kitley, Ontario, on 25 October 1819. [PAO.MS154]

MURPHY, ..., formerly a private of the York Chasseurs, settled in Drummond, Ontario, on 1 October 1819. [PAO.MS154]

MURPHY, ..., formerly Quartermaster of the Prince of York's Chasseurs, settled in Bathurst, Ontario, on 7 October 1819. [PAO.MS154]

MURRAINE, JOHN, born in Ireland during, jailed in Chester on suspicion of being a runaway indentured servant 4 March 1785. [PaGaz#2864]

MURRAY, ANDREW, from Drogheda, a butcher and indentured servant, absconded from his master William Weston, 5th Street, Philadelphia, 29 May 1775. [Penn.Ledger#19]

MURRAY, JAMES, a laborer, an indentured servant, who immigrated from Ireland on the Favorite, master Robert Alcorn, to Philadelphia in July 1784. [PaGaz#2832]

MURRAY, WILLIAM, late Sergeant of the Canadian Fencibles, settled in Beckwith, Ontario, on 26 November 1819. [PAO.MS154]

NARRY, BARTHOLEMEW, born 1803, [brother of Patrick Narry who sailed in the Roscius, Captain Eldridge.], son Michael born 1822, and brother William born 1812, from Ballykilcline, Kilglass parish, County Roscommon, emigrated from Liverpool on 13 April 1848 on the Channing, Captain Huttleston, to New York, arrived there 17 April 1848 [AH22/345]

NARRY, PATRICK, born 1807, wife Mary born 1819, with daughter Bridget born 1846, from Ballykilcline, Kilglass parish, County Roscommon, emigrated from Liverpool on 19 September 1847 on the Roscius, Captain Eldridge, to New York, arrived there 21 October 1847 [AH22/345]

NASH, MARTIN, from Goran, County Kilkenny, former soldier of the 37th Regiment, settled at Rideau, Canada, 1820. [PAC:RG8.B22894/49]

NEAL, LAWRENCE, born in Ireland during 1745, absconded from John Townsend in Chester County, Pennsylvania, on 20 August 1769. [PaGaz#2122]

NEARY, MARY, born 1812, son James born 1844, and daughter Anne born 1840, with brother-in-law John born 1831, sister-in-law Bridget born 1834, and sister-in-law Catherine born 1823, from Ballykilcline, Kilglass parish, County Roscommon, emigrated from Liverpool on 18 October 1847 on the Creole, Captain Rattoone, to New York, arrived there 22 November 1847 [AH22/345]

NEEL, JOHN, born in Ireland during 1765, a cooper and indentured servant who absconded from John Maxwell, Caernarvon, Lancaster County, Pennsylvania, April 1785. [PaGaz#2865]

NESBIT, THOMAS, arrived from Belfast on the Dusley Galley, Captain Hamilton, in 1753, sought in Pennsylvania on 19 May 1765. [PaJ#1172]

NESBIT, THOMAS, born in Ireland during 1771, a farmer, arrived in Waldboro, USA, late 1821, on the ship Lydia, Captain Adams. [USNA]

NEVEL, FRANCIS, absconded from Soloman Ridgway in Burlington County, West New Jersey, on 10 April 1769. [PaGaz#2109]

NEVENS, EDWARD. born in Ireland during in 1759, absconded from Samuel Moody, Salsbury, Lancaster County, Pennsylvania, on 10 March 1777. [PaEP#331]

NEVISTON, WILLIAM, son of John Neviston late of Ireland, indented for 8 years service in Virginia on 25 July 1685. [CLRO/AIA#14/341]

NEWELL, JONAS, born in Ireland during in 1771, a shoemaker, with Mary born in Ireland during 1774, and 8 children, arrived in Philadelphia in late 1821 on the ship William and Jane, Captain Brown. [USNA]

NIXON, ROBERT, an Irish house-carpenter, former apprentice to Thomas Simpson in Drogheda, sought in Philadelphia on 7 October 1783. [PIG#102]

NOLAN, JOHN, with his wife, son and daughter, settled in Beckwith, Ontario, on 28 December 1819. [PAO.MS154]

NOONAN, WILLIAM, born in Ireland during in 1743, absconded from John Townsend in Chester County, Pennsylvania, on 20 August 1769. [PaGaz#2122]

NOWLER, PATRICK, born in Ireland during in 1767, an indentured servant who absconded from Caleb Lippencott in Northampton, Burlington, New Jersey, on 19 May 1786. [PaGaz#2923]

O'BRADY, OWEN, born in Ireland during in 1765, an indentured servant who absconded from Edward Edair in Philadelphia in March 1785. [PEH#7]

O'BRIAN, JOSEPH H., with his wife and daughter, settled in Elmsley and Beckwith, Ontario, on 1 November 1816. [PAO.MS154]

O'BRIAN, MATTHEW, born in County Dublin, settled in Baltimore, Maryland, pro.26 September 1815 Baltimore [Wills Liber 10, fo.73.]

O'BRYEN, JOHN, born in 1778, enlisted in the British Army in County Mayo during 1813, discharged in St John 1818, settled in Dalhousie, Nova Scotia, in 1820. [PRO.WO.25#548]

O'CONNOR, ...,possibly late of the York Chasseurs, settled in Drummond, Ontario, on 1 October 1819. [PAO.MS154]

O'CONNOR, MICHAEL, born in Ireland during in 1810, settled in Cherokee County, Georgia, by 1850. [1850 Census]

O'CONNOR, MORRIS, born in Ireland during in 1810, settled in Cherokee County, Georgia, by 1850. [1850 Census]

O'DONNELL, MICHAEL, born in Ireland during in 1781, a farmer, with Mary O'Donnell born in Ireland during in 1786, arrived in Waldboro, in late 1821 on the Lydia, Captain Adams. [USNA]

O'HARA, THOMAS, late of the Glengarry Fencibles, settled in Burgess, Ontario, on 26 September 1816. [PAO.MS154]

O'MONY, ROGER, an Irish indentured servant who absconded from his master Bryan Reilly and John Carmichael, in March 1775. [SCGaz#60]

O'NEAL, BERNARD, born 1802, wife Betty born 1807, sons Bernard born 1834 and John born 1831, and daughter Anne born 1827, from Ballykilcline, Kilglass parish, County Roscommon, emigrated from Liverpool on 26 September 1847 on the Metoka to New York, arrived there 30 October 1847 [AH22/345]

O'NEAL, JOHN, born in Ireland during around 1750, a runaway servant from Lawrence Salter, Airston Forge, Evesham, Burlington County, in 1774. [Pa.Gaz.#2405]

O'NEIL, CONSTANTINE, with his wife, 2 sons and 3 daughters, arrived in Canada via USA, settled in Beckwith, Ontario, on 30 November 1815. [PAO.MS154]

O'NEILL, JAMES, a tanner, absconded from the Three Brothers, John McClellan, in Philadelphia in October 1784. [PaGaz#2838]

O'NEILL, JOHN, born in Ireland during in 1753, absconded from Henry Snevely in Leacock township, Lancaster County, Pennsylvania, on 16 July 1769. [PaGaz#2120]

O'NEILL, JOHN, from Londonderry to Philadelphia on the Faithful Steward, shipwrecked off the Capes of Delaware in January 1786. [PEH#100]

O'NEILL, PATRICK, born in 1797, enlisted in the British Army in County Tipperary in 1813, discharged in Fredericton during 1818, settled in Dalhousie, Nova Scotia, in 1820. [PRO.WO.25#548]

O'NEILL, WILLIAM, born in 1774, enlisted in the British Army in Kilkenny in 1805, discharged in St John, Newfoundland, during 1818, settled in Dalhousie, Nova Scotia, in 1820. [PRO.WO.25#548]

O'NELIS, CONNEL, born during 1754 in Ireland, an indentured servant who absconded from Thomas Strawbridge, Londonderry township, Chester County, Pennsylvania, on 27 April 1772. [PaGaz.#2263]

O'SHONACHY, THOMAS, alias BRYAN, aged over 30, absconded from Joseph Richardson in Providence township, Philadelphia, on 13 March 1769. [PaGaz#2100]

ORAN, ..., former Sergeant of the York Chasseurs, settled in Drummond, Ontario, on 1 October 1819. [PAO.MS154]

ORR, HUGH, born in 1744, an Irish servant who absconded from John Rankin, New Garden township, Chester County, Pennsylvania, in April 1772. [PaGaz.#2260]

ORR, JAMES, born in Ireland during in 1781, a farmer with 3 children, arrived in Waldboro in late 1821 on the ship Lydia, Captain Adams. [USNA]

PADIAN, RICHARD, born 1815, wife Mary born 1817, sons James born 1838 and William born 1835, with daughters Bridget born 1837 and Maria born 1841, from Ballykilcline, Kilglass parish, County Roscommon, emigrated from Liverpool on 19 September 1847 on the Roscius, Captain Eldridge, to New York, arrived there 21 October 1847 [AH22/345]

PARK, WILLIAM, born in Ireland during in 1800, a farmer, arrived in Waldboro, USA, late 1821, on the ship Lydia, Captain Adams. [USNA]

PARKER, LAURENCE, late private of the Glengarry Fencibles, settled in Drummond, Ontario, on 16 July 1816. [PAO.MS154]

PARKINSON, JOHN, born in Ireland during in 1783, a shoemaker who absconded from William Blake, a cordiner in Talbot County, Maryland, on 13 May 1785. [PaJ#1803]

PATTERSON, WILLIAM born in northern Ireland in 1763, a blacksmith and an indentured servant who absconded from John Clark, blacksmith in Baltimore, in July 1786. [PHGA#172]

PERCIVAL, ROBERT, with his wife, 2 sons and 3 daughters, arrived in Canada on the Betty and Mary on 20 August 1815, settled in Beckwith, Ontario, on 9 December 1815. [PAO.MS154]

PERRY, JANE, born in Ireland during in 1791, a spinster, arrived in Newport, USA, late 1821 on the ship Belle Savage, master Russell. [USNA]

POKE, JAMES, born in Ireland during in 1766, a runaway indentured servant jailed in Chester on 13 October 1785. [PaGaz#2892]

POOLE, QUENTIN, emigrated from Belfast on the Prince George, master R. Beatty, arrived on 7 December 1768. [GaGaz#271]

PORTER, ALEXANDER, born in Ireland during 1765, an indentured servant who absconded from James Boyd in Sedsbury, Chester County, Pennsylvania, on 24 January 1785. [PaGaz#2852]

PORTER, JAMES, arrived in Canada via USA, settled in Drummond, Ontario, on 25 November 1815. [PAO.MS154]

POTTER, PATRICK, born in Ireland during 1815, settled in Cherokee County, Georgia, by 1850. [1850 Census]

POWER, ROBERT, arrived in Canada on the brig John on 3 September 1815, settled in Beckwith, Ontario, on 9 December 1815. [PAO.MS154]

POWER, WILLIAM, an indentured servant, who immigrated from Ireland on the Favourite, master Robert Alcorn, to Philadelphia in July 1784. [PaGaz#2832]

POWER, WILLIAM, arrived in Canada on the Mary Ann on 8 August 1817, settled in Beckwith on 4 September 1817. [PAO.MS154]

PREGAN, WILLIAM, born 1749, a whitesmith in Strabane, County Tyrone, an indentured servant who emigrated from Londonderry to Philadelphia on the Rose in June 1772, absconded from James Little, Southwark, Philadelphia, 25 August 1772. [PaGaz.#2280]

PRICE, GEORGE, born 1802, from Bassett's Bridge, Kilkenny, died on Tulloch Estate, Jamaica, on 15 April 188-. [Spanish Town g/s, Jamaica]

QUIGLEY, JAMES, late Sergeant of the Glengarry Regiment, settled in Drummond, Ontario, on 16 July 1816. [PAO.MS154]

QUINN, CATHERINE, born 1817, sons Hugh born 1841, James born 1839, and James born 1846, daughter Anne born 1844, with Catherine Quinn born 1830, from Ballykilcline, Kilglass parish, County Roscommon, emigrated from Liverpool on 18 October 1847 on the Creole, Captain Rattoone, to New York, arrived there 22 November 1847 [AH22/345]

QUINN, JOHN, born in Ireland during 1763, an indentured servant who absconded from Robert Dixon, Chuptank Bridge, Pennsylvania, 21 November 1784. [PaGaz#2844]

QUINN, PATRICK, born in Ireland during ca.1729, absconded from Hugh Bowes in Philadelphia on 7 April 1769. [PaGaz#2109]

QUINN, PETER C., born in Ireland during 1803, a farmer, arrived in Waldboro, USA, late 1821 on the ship Lydia, Captain Adams. [USNA]

QULTY, JOHN, born 1775, enlisted in the British Army in Limerick 1804, discharged in St John, 1818, settled in Dalhousie, Nova Scotia, 1820. [PRO.WO.25#548]

RAE, PATRICK, a tailor and Irish indented servant, absconded from Caleb Pierce in Newton, Chester County, Pennsylvania, on 9 July 1786. [PaGaz#2928]

RALSTON, WILLIAM, born in Ireland during 1740, a blacksmith, arrived in America 1766, absconded from Thomas White in Oxford, Chester County, Pennsylvania, in July 1769. [PaGaz#2118]

RALSTONE, WILLIAM, born in Ireland during, a weaver and indentured servant who absconded from James Adams in Warwick, Bucks County, Pennsylvania, 7 May 1785. [PaGaz#2868]

RAPH, JOSEPH, with his wife, 3 sons and 1 daughter, arrived in Canada on the Sally and Tom, settled in Edwardsburgh, Ontario, on 5 August 1817. [PAO.MS154]

READ, ANN, born in Ireland during in 1769, an indentured servant who absconded from William Mecum in Lower Penn's Neck, County Salem, in July 1785. [PaGaz#2881]

READ, JAMES, born 1751, a mason, arrived from Waterford on the snow Charlotte in July 1774, an Irish runaway servant from William Ball's Plantation, near Glass House, Kensington, near Philadelphia, on 30. October 1774. [Pa.Gaz.#2402]

READ, GEORGE KANE, settled in Edwardsburgh, Ontario, on 25 October 1819. [PAO.MS154]

REDMOND, JOHN, and his wife, arrived in Canada on the Prince Asturias on 4 June 1817, settled in Yonge, Ontario, on 15 August 1817.[PAO.MS154]

REDMOND, STEPHEN, arrived in Canada on the Golden Grove on 19 August 1815, settled in Beckwith, Ontario, on 13 December 1815.[PAO.MS154]

REED, MICHAEL, born in Ireland during 1765, an indentured servant who absconded from Jacob Jeanes in Moreland, Montgomery County, on 30 November 1785. [PaGaz#2900]

REID, JAMES, settled in Newcastle Ontario, on 19 June 1819. [PAO.MS154]

REILEY, MICHAEL, born in Ireland during, a tanner, absconded from George Githens, Cole's Town, Burlington County, New Jersey, in March 1785. [PaJ#1798]

REYNOLDS, BRIDGET, born 1787, sons James born 1819, John born 1823, and Joseph born 1825, with Thomas born 1807, Bridget born 1833, and Catherine born 1845, from Ballykilcline, Kilglass parish, County Roscommon, emigrated from Liverpool on 19 September 1847 on the Roscius, Captain Eldridge, to New York, arrived there 21 October 1847 [AH22/346]

REYNOLDS, MICHAEL, born 1838, from Ballykilcline, Kilglass parish, County Roscommon, emigrated from Liverpool on 13 March 1848 on the Channing, Captain Huttleston, to New York, arrived there 17 April 1848. [AH22/346]

REYNOLDS, PATRICK, born in Ireland during 1765, an indentured servant who absconded from Francis Dawes and James Bryson in Baltimore, Maryland, on 16 September 1784. [PaGaz#2835]

REYNOLDS, THOMAS, from Londonderry to Philadelphia on the Faithful Steward, shipwrecked off the Capes of Delaware in January 1786. [PEH#100]

REYNOLDS, THOMAS, born 1814, wife Mary born 1818, sons Andrew born 1843, James born 1840, John born 1842, Thomas born 1846, infant daughter Mary, brother Andrew born 1821, and mother Bridget born 1788, from Ballykilcline, Kilglass parish, County Roscommon, emigrated from Liverpool on 26 September 1848 on the Metoka to New York, arrived there 30 October 1848. [AH22/346]

RICE, PATRICK, late private of the Glengarry Fencibles, settled in Drummond, Ontario, on 16 July 1816. [PAO.MS154]

RICHARDS, EDWARD, arrived in Canada on the Betty and Mary on 20 August 1815, settled in Drummond, Ontario, on 19 November 1815. [PAO.MS154]

RICHARDS, RICHARD, with his wife, son and 3 daughters, arrived in Canada via USA, settled in Drummond, Ontario, on 21 May 1817. [PAO.MS154]

RILEY, ELEANOR, born in Ireland during in 1766, an indentured servant who absconded from John Hill in Middletown, Chester County, on 11 June 1786. [PaGaz#2926]

ROBERT, MATTHEW, with his wife, 3 sons and 1 daughter, arrived in Canada on the Mary, on 20 July 1817, settled in Oxford, Ontario, on 9 September 1817. [PAO.MS154]

ROBERTSON, JAMES, born in Ireland during in 1748, absconded from Joseph Fallows, Pennsgrove Forge, Chester County, Pennsylvania, on 9 October 1772. [PaGaz.#2278]

ROBERTSON, NANCY, born in Ireland during in 1763, an indentured servant who absconded from William Neston in Warwick, Bucks County, Pennsylvania, in October 1785. [PaGaz#2893]

ROBESON, JOHN, born in Ireland during in 1747, absconded from Alexander Lowry in Donegal, Lancaster County, Pennsylvania, in August 1769. [PaGaz#2120]

ROBINSON, HENRY, arrived in Newcastle, Delaware, from Londonderry on the brig Mary in November 1789. [Pa.Pkt, 5.12.1789]

ROBINSON, JAMES, late of the Prince of York's Chasseurs, settled in Bathurst, Ontario, on 21 October 1819. [PAO.MS154]

RODENHAM, CHARLES, born in Ireland during 1820, settled in Carroll County, Georgia, by 1850. [1850 Census]

ROSS, JANE, born in Ireland during 1781, with 4 children, arrived in Newport, USA, late 1821 on the ship Belle Savage, Captain Russell. [USNA]

ROWSON, EDWARD, with his wife, son and daughter, arrived in Canada on the Mary and Betty on 19 September 1816, settled in Beckwith, Ontario, on 1 January 1817. [PAO.MS154]

RUCKLE, HENRY, with his wife, 2 sons and 1 daughter, arrived in Canada via USA, settled in Drummond, Ontario, on 9 December 1815. [PAO.MS154]

RUSHFORD, GEORGE, from Londonderry to Philadelphia on the Faithful Steward, shipwrecked off the Capes of Delaware in January 1786. [PEH#100]

RYAN, MICHAEL, born in Ireland during 1764, an indentured servant who absconded from Francis Dawes and James Bryson in Baltimore, Maryland, on 16 September 1784. [PaGaz#2835]

RYAN, PETER, a tobacconist, an indentured servant, who immigrated from Ireland on the Favourite, master Robert Alcorn, to Philadelphia in July 1784. [PaGaz#2832]

RYNE, JOHN, born in Ireland during ca.1746, absconded from Thomas Morton, Mooretown, Burlington County, West New Jersey, in May 1769. [PaGaz#2111]

SCHARP, JAMES, Old Leighton, County Carlow, settled at Rideau, Canada, in 1820. [PAC:RG8.B22894]

SCHARP, THOMAS, Castlecomer, County Kilkennry, settled at Rideau, Canada, in 1820. [PAC:RG8.B22894/49]

SCOTT, JOHN, from Londonderry to Philadelphia on the Faithful Steward, shipwrecked off the Capes of Delaware in January 1786. [PEH#100]

SCOTT, REBECCA, born in Ireland during 1778, with 2 children, arrived in Waldboro, USA, late 1821 on the ship Lydia, Captain Adams. [USNA]

SCOTT, THOMAS, arrived in Newcastle, Delaware, from Londonderry on the brig Mary in November 1789. [Pa.Pkt, 5.12.1789]

SCULLY, JOHN, born in Ireland during 1747, an indentured servant who absconded from the brig Hawk, master Bennet Matthews, when it arrived in Philadelphia from Waterford on 18 June 1769. [PaGaz#2114]

SERGEANT, JOHN, born in Ireland during 1801, a farmer, arrived in Waldboro, USA, late 1821 on the ship Lydia, Captain Adams. [USNA]

SHANNON, WILLIAM, born in the north of Ireland 1745, absconded from John Schellenberg in Salisbury township, Lancaster County, Pennsylvania, on 10 August 1769. [PaGaz#2120]

SHARP, ANDREW, born in Ireland during 1766, a blacksmith and indentured servant, immigrated on the Mary, Captain Stevenson, from Londonderry in 1783, absconded from James Hill in East Nottingham, Chester County, Pennsylvania, in June 1784. [PaGaz#2827]

SHAW, DENNY, from Ireland, indented for 4 years service in Jamaica on 28 April 1685. [CLRO/AIA#14/228]

SHAW, JOHN, from Londonderry to Philadelphia on the Faithful Steward, shipwrecked off the Capes of Delaware in January 1786. [PEH#100]

SHEARER, JAMES, born 1762, arrived in Philadelphia in 1787 from Ireland on the Friendship, Captain McCadden, an indentured servant who absconded from Thomas Cummins in East Whiteland, Chester County, Pennsylvania, on 6 August 1787. [PaGaz#2985]

SHEHAWN, THOMAS, indentured servant from Youghall, County Cork, to Maryland on the Increase, master Philip Poppleston, assigned to William Sharp in Talbot County, Maryland, 1677[Md. Patents, Liber 20, fo.184]

SHEELINE, JOHN, born 1751, an Irish servant who absconded from John Evans and Joseph Jenkins, Carnarvon township, Lancaster County, Pennsylvania, in August 1772. [PaGaz.#2278]

SIMPSON, WILLIAM, born in Sligo in 1832, LRCSI, died at Black River, Jamaica, on 21 July 1867. [St Elizabeth parish g/s, Jamaica]

SMITH, JAMES, from Londonderry to Philadelphia on the Faithful Steward, shipwrecked off the Capes of Delaware in January 1786. [PEH#100]

SMITH, MICHAEL, born in Ireland during, jailed in Chester, Pennsylvania, suspected of being a runaway indentured servant, on 23 June 1784. [PaGaz#2828]

SMITH, STEPHEN, late of the Prince of York's Chasseurs, settled in Bathurst, Ontario, on 21 October 1819. [PAO.MS154]

SMITH, THOMAS, indentured servant from Youghall, County Cork, to Maryland on the Increase, master Philip Poppleston, assigned to William Sharp in Talbot County, Maryland, 1677 [MHR Patents, Liber 20, fo.184]

SMITH, WILLIAM, born in Ireland during, jailed in Chester, Pennsylvania, suspeted of being a runaway indentured servant, on 23 June 1784. [Pa Gaz#2828]

SMYTH, JAMES, a smith, an indentured servant, who immigrated from Ireland on the Favourite, master Robert Alcorn, to Philadelphia in July 1784. [PaGaz#2832]

SINCLAIR, ALEXANDER, an Irish indentured servant who absconded from his masters Bryan Reilly and James Carmichael, in March 1775. [SCGaz#60]

SOMERVILLE, WILLIAM, arrived in Canada via USA, settled in Bathurst, Ontario, on 16 November 1815. [PAO.MS154]

SPEARIN, NICHOLAS, born in Ireland during 1803, settled in Cherokee County, Georgia, by 1850. [1850 Census]

SPEIRS, JOHN, from Londonderry to Philadelphia on the Faithful Steward, shipwrecked off the Capes of Delaware in January 1786. [PEH#100]

STACEY, WILLIAM, arrived in Canada on the Betty and Mary on 20 August 1815, settled in Drummond, Ontario, on 30 November 1815. [PAO.MS154]

STAPLES, RICHARD, settled in Cavan township, Newcastle district, Ontario, on 15 October 1819. [PAO.MS154]

STEDMAN, FRANCIS, with his wife, son and 2 daughters, arrived in Canada on the Mary Ann Bell, on 9 July 1817, settled in Drummond, Ontario, on 9 August 1817. [PAO.MS154]

STEDMAN, NATHANIEL, arrived in Canada on the Betty and Mary on 20 August 1814, settled in Drummond, Ontario, on 14 November 1815. [PAO.MS154]

STEDMAN, WILLIAM, arrived in Canada on the Betty and Mary on 20 August 1814, settled in Drummond, Ontario, on 14 November 1815. [PAO.MS154]

STEVENSON, ANDREW, born in Ireland during, emigrated to America in 1775, master of the American ship Beaver in Glasgow during August 1802. [SRO.CE60.11.31.862]

STEWART, ANDREW, arrived in Newcastle, Delaware, from Londonderry on the brig Mary in November 1789. [Pa.Pkt, 5.12.1789]

STEWART, ANNE, born 1798, wife of Francis Stewart, son John born 1818 from Ballykilcline, Kilglass parish, County Roscommon, emigrated from Liverpool on 13 March 1848 on the Channing, Captain Huttleston, to New York, arrived there 17 April 1848. [AH22/346]

STEWART, BRIDGET, born 1813, sons James born 1831 and Michael born 1843, and daughter born 1834, from Ballykilcline, Kilglass parish, County Roscommon, emigrated from Liverpool on 13 March 1848 on the Channing, Captain Huttleston, to New York, arrived there 17 April 1848. [AH22/346]

STEWART, FRANCIS, born 1792, from Ballykilcline, Kilglass parish, County Roscommon, emigrated from Dublin on 16 March 1848 on the Laconic to New York. [AH22/346]

STUART, GEORGE, born 1807, wife Bridget born 1815, sons Charles born 1841 and John born 1843, daughter Mary born 1837, from Ballykilcline, Kilglass parish, County Roscommon, emigrated from Liverpool on 18 October 1847 on the Creole, Captain Rattoone, to New York, arrived 22 November 1847. [AH22/346]

STUART, JAMES, born 1784, wife Ellen born 1787, son George born 1827, daughter Ellen born 1829, from Ballykilcline, Kilglass parish, County Roscommon, emigrated from Liverpool on 19 September 1847 on the Roscius, Captain Eldridge, to New York, arrived there 21 October 1847. [AH22/346]

STUART, JOHN, born 1826, sisters Bridget born 1830 and Catherine born 1832, from Ballykilcline, Kilglass parish, County Roscommon, emigrated from Liverpool on 18 October 1847 on the Creole, Captain Rattoone, to New York, arrived there 22 November 1847. [AH22/346]

STUART, PATRICK, born 1829, sister Catherine born 1822, from Ballykilcline, Kilglass parish, County Roscommon, emigrated from Liverpool on 19 September 1847 on the Roscius, Captain Eldridge, to New York, arrived there 21 October 1847. [AH22/346]

STUART, WILLIAM, born 1800, wife Bridget born 1804, sons Charles born 1833, Michael born 1835, and William born 1839, daughter Eliza born 1837, from Ballykilcline, Kilglass parish, County Roscommon, emigrated from Liverpool on 18 October 1847 on the Creole, Captain Rattoone, to New York, arrived there 22 November 1847. [AH22/347]

STUNKARD, JAMES, from Londonderry to Philadelphia on the Faithful Steward, shipwrecked off the Capes of Delaware in January 1786. [PEH#100]

SWAYNE, JOSEPH, settled in Cavan township, Newcastle district, Ontario, on 15 October 1819. [PAO.MS154]

SWENEY, JOHN, born in Ireland during, a tailor and an indentured servant who absconded from Jacob Walker in Radnor, Chester County, Pennsylvania, on 10 April 1785. [PaGaz#2863]

TAGGART, WILLIAM, born in Ireland during 1792, a farmer, arrived in Philadelphia late 1821 on the ship William and Jane, Captain Brown. [USNA]

TAYLOR, CLAUDIUS, born in Ireland during 1742, a carpenter, absconded from Edward Bonsall, in May 1765. [PaJ#1172]

TAYLOR, JOHN, from Rosona, Tipperary, settled at Rideau, Canada, in 1820. [PAC:RG8.B22894/49]

THOMPSON, ANDREW, arrived in Newcastle, Delaware, from Londonderry on the brig Mary in November 1789. [Pa.Pkt, 5.12.1789]

THOMPSON, JOHN, former soldier of the 8th Regiment, settled in Burgess, Ontario, on 22 August 1816. [PAO.MS154]

THOMPSON, JOHN, late of the 8th Regiment, settled in Burgess, Ontario, on 22 August 1816. [PAO.MS154]

THOMPSON, MATTHEW, born 1799 in Strabane, County Tyrone, '35 years in Jamaica', died on 22 August 1853. [St Thomas parish g/s, Jamaica]

THOMSON, SARAH, born 1712, daughter of ... Thomson in Lurgan, County Armagh, sought in Philadelphia in June 1769. [PaGaz#2115]

THOMPSON, HUGH, arrived in Newcastle, Delaware, from Londonderry on the brig Mary in November 1789. [Pa.Pkt, 5.12.1789]

THORNTON, GEORGE, born in Ireland during 1762, an indentured servant who absconded from Thomas Bull in Chester County on 14 November 1785. [PaGaz#2895]

TOLERTON, M., born in Ireland during 1801, a farmer, arrived in Waldboro, USA, late 1821 on the ship Lydia, Captain Adams. [USNA]

TONNEY, DANIEL, born in Ireland during, an indentured servant who absconded in Bucks County, Pennsylvania, on 22 August 1785. [PaGaz#2882]

TOOL, PATRICK, born 1767, an indentured servant who absconded from Job Coles in Gloucester County on 26 March 1786. [PaGaz#2913]

TIVVY, SARAH, born in Ireland during in 1760, an indentured servant who absconded from Peter Jacquet jr. at Christiana Ferry, Newcastle County, Delaware, in August 1785. [PaGaz#2883]

WAKEFIELD, DANIEL, arrived in Newcastle, Delaware, from Londonderry on the brig Mary in November 1789. [Pa.Pkt, 5.12.1789]

WALL, JAMES, born in Ireland during 1753, absconded from Henry Diets in Upper Salford township, Philadelphia county, on 16 April 1769. [PaGaz#2105]

WALL, JOHN P., born 1775 in Ireland, a merchant, arrived in Newport, USA, on the brig Monitor, Captain Whitton, late 1821. [USNA]

WALLACE, ALEXANDER, emigrated to New York, a merchant there, a Loyalist in 1776. [ANY.I.127]

WALLACE, HUGH, emigrated to New York in 1752, a merchant there, member of HM Council of New York 1769, Loyalist in 1776, returned to Waterford, Ireland, died in December 1787. [ANY.I.127]

WALLACE, THOMAS, late private of the Glengarry Regiment, settled in Drummond, Ontario, on 18 July 1816. [PAO.MS154]

WARD, PATRICK, born in Ireland during 1787, a farmer, arrived in New York late 1821 on the Dublin Packet, Captain Newcomb. [USNA]

WATSON, ROBERT, arrived in Philadelphia from Londonderry on the brig Conyngham, master Robert Conyngham on 1 August 1789. [Pa.Pkt.11.8.1789]

WATT, ANDREW, from Londonderry to Philadelphia on the Faithful Steward, shipwrecked off the Capes of Delaware in January 1786. [PEH#100]

WEBSTER, THOMAS, settled in Cavan township, Newcastle district, Ontario, on 21 September 1818. [PAO.MS154]

WELSH, DAVID, an Irish indentured servant who absconded from James Brown and Richard Strode in West Bradford, Chester County, Pennsylvania, on 12 June 1786. [PaGaz#2923]

WELCH, MICHAEL, born in Ireland during, jailed in Chester, Pennsylvania, on 8 February 1785. [PaGaz#2854]

WELSH, JOHN, born in Ireland during 1796, a teacher, arrived in Newberryport, USA, late 1821. [USNA]

WELSH, SARAH, born in Dublin 1748, immigrated into Philadelphia on the Two Friends, master William Cronitch, an indentured servant who absconded from William Adam in 1784. [PaGaz#2822]

WHITE, GEORGE, born in Ireland during 1801, a farmer, arrived in Philadelphia late 1821 on the brig Rising Sun, Captain Prince. [USNA]

WHITE, JOHN, arrived in Canada on the Betty and Mary on 20 August 1814, settled in Drummond, Ontario, on 14 November 1815. [PAO.MS154]

WILLIAMS, BARNER, born in Ireland during 1745, absconded from the armed schooner Delaware of Pennsylvania, in March 1777. [PaEP#331]

WILLIAMS, JOHN, born in Ireland during 1745, a shoemaker, absconded from Samuel Cheeseman, in January 1766. [Pa.J#1205]

WILLIAMS, THOMAS, an Irish servant who absconded from Valentine Vanboy, Lower Merion, Pennsylvania, in April 1772. [PaGaz.#2260]

WILLIAMS, WILLIAM, an Irish baker, who absconded from James Forsyth, Conogichig, Chambersburgh, Pennsylvania, in May 1765. [PaJ#1171]

WILLIAMS, WILLIAM, born 1755 in Ireland, an apprentice who absconded from Conrad Aloter in Philadelphia in August 1772. [PaGaz.#2280]

WILSON, DAVID, born in Ireland during 1786, a farmer, with Eleanor born in Ireland during 1793, and 2 children, arrived in Waldboro, USA, late 1821 on the ship Lydia, Captain Adams. [USNA]

WILSON, HUGH, born in Ireland during 1770, an indentured servant who absconded from Stephen Love in Horsham, Montgomery County, on 2 July 1787. [PaGaz#2982]

WILSON, JAMES, born in Ireland during 1796, a carpenter, arrived in Philadelphia in late 1821. [USNA]

WILSON, JOHN, with his wife, son and 2 daughters, arrived in Canada on the Mary on 20 July 1817, settled in Drummond, Ontario, on 11 September 1817. [PAO.MS154]

WILSON, JOSEPH, born in Ireland during 1796, a laborer, arrived in Oswegatchie, USA, late 1821 on the boat Huron, master Graham. [USNA]

WILSON, JOSEPH, born in Ireland during 1802, a farmer, arrived in Philadelphia late 1821. [USNA]

WILSON, Mrs MATILDA, born in Dublin during 1769, emigrated via Greenock to America, naturalised in New York on 16 November 1818.

WILSON, NANCY, born in Ireland during 1754, arrived in Waldboro, USA, late 1821 on the ship Lydia, Captain Adams. [USNA]

WINSHALL, JOSEPH, born in Ireland during 1791, a carpenter, with his wife Fanny born in Ireland during 1797, and their children, arrived in Oswegatchie, USA, late 1821 on the boat Huron, Captain Graham. [USNA]

WINTER, HONOR, born 1787, son Thomas born 1817, daughters Honor born 1829 and Margaret born 1823, with Catherine born 1846, from Ballykilcline, Kilglass parish, County Roscommon, emigrated from Liverpool on 26 September 1847 on the Metoka to New York, arrived there 30 October 1847. [AH22/347]

WOODS, JAMES, late of the Glengarry Fencibles, settled in Drummond, Ontario, on 16 July 1816. [PAO.MS154]

WRIGHT, Mrs CAROLINE, born in Ireland during 1810, settled in Carroll County, Georgia, by 1850. [1850 Census]

WRIGHT, SAMUEL, from Londonderry to Philadelphia on the Faithful Steward, shipwrecked off the Capes of Delaware in January 1786. [PEH#100]

WRIGHT, WILLIAM, arrived in Canada on the Alexander on 1 April 1817, settled in Bathurst, Ontario, on 30 June 1817. [PAO.MS154]

WYNNE, BRIDGET, born 1818, from Ballykilcline, Kilglass parish, County Roscommon, emigrated from Liverpool on 13 March 1848 on the Channing, Captain Huttleston, to New York, arrived there 17 April 1848. [AH22/347]

WYNNE, JOHN, born 1795, son Patrick born 1825, daughter Mary born 1834, from Ballykilcline, Kilglass parish, County Roscommon, emigrated from Liverpool on 26 September 1847 on the Metoka to New York, arrived there 30 October 1847. [AH22/347]

WYNNE, MICHAEL, born 1788, wife Bell born 1793, son James born 1832, daughters Catherine born 1835 and Mary born 1830, from Ballykilcline, Kilglass parish, County Roscommon, emigrated from Liverpool on 13 March 1848 on the Channing, Captain Huttleston, to New York, arrived there 17 April 1848. [AH22/347]

YORK, JOHN, from Londonderry to Philadelphia on the Faithful Steward, shipwrecked off the Capes of Delaware in January 1786. [PEH#100]

YOUNG, THOMAS, a sawyer, an indentured servant, who immigrated from Ireland on the Favourite, master Robert Alcorn, to Philadelphia in July 1784. [PaGaz#2832]

"Just arrived from Ireland the brig Patty, master Robert Hardie, having aboard about 100 servants - men, women, boys and girls, among which are sundry tradesmen such as smiths, nailmakers, shoemakers, taylors, skinners, carpenters, gardeners, grooms and farmers whose times are to be disposed of by the master on board the said brig lying off the Drawbridge, or Andrew Don at the house of Nathaniel Donnell in Front Street."

PaGaz#2262, 30 April 1772

REFERENCES

ARCHIVES

CLRO	=	City of London Record Office
MHR	=	Maryland Hall of Records, Annapolis
NEHGS	=	New England Historic Genealogy Society
PAC	=	Public Archives of Canada
PAO	=	Public Archives of Ontario
PCC	=	Prerogative Court of Canterbury
PRO	=	Public Record Office, London
SRO	=	Scottish Record Office, Edinburgh
USNA	=	United States National Archives

PUBLICATIONS

AH	=	Analecta Hibernica, series
AJ	=	Aberdeen Journal, series
ANY	=	Bio. Reg. of St Andrews Society of New York
CalSPIre.	=	Calendar of State Papers, Ireland, series
GG	=	Matriculation Albums of Glasgow University
NSHR	=	Nova Scotia Historical Review, series
PaEP	=	Philadelphia Evening Post, series
PaGaz	=	Philadelphia Gazette, series
PaJ	=	Philadelphia Journal, series
PaPkt	=	Pennsylvania Packet, series
PEH	=	Pennsylvania Evening Herald, series
PIG	=	Independent Gazetteer, Philadelphia, series
PL	=	Pennsylvania Ledger, series
SCGaz	=	South Carolina Gazette, series
SPAWI	=	Cal. of State Papers, America & West Indies, series

IRISH EMIGRANTS

IN

NORTH AMERICA

PART FIVE

by David Dobson

INTRODUCTION

Emigration from Ireland to the Americas can be said to have started in earnest during the early eighteenth century. In 1718 the first successful emigration from Ireland to New England occurred which laid the foundations for the large-scale settlement of colonial America by the "Scotch-Irish". There had been groups of Irish settlers during the seventeenth century, some involuntary, in the West Indies. The earliest attempt, albeit unsuccessful, to emigrate from Ireland to New England was that of a group aboard the *Eaglewing* in the 1630s. Some early emigrants went as indentured servants, often via ports such as Bristol and London. The scale of emigration, particularly from the north of Ireland, grew from a trickle in 1718 to a torrent in the mid-nineteenth century. Specific groups of emigrants have attracted the attention of researchers such as Frances McDonnell who has identified felons and criminals involuntarily transported to America, in her Emigrants from Ireland to America 1735-1743 (Baltimore, 1992). Ira Glazier and Michael Tepper list tens of thousands who were forced to seek refuge in America during and after the potato famine 1846-1851 in The Famine Immigrants (Baltimore, 1984-).

This book is based mainly on contemporary newspapers and archival sources in Canada and the United States.

David Dobson
St Andrews, Scotland
1999

IRELAND
To illustrate the reign of James II
English Miles
0 10 20 30 40 50
10
9
8
7
6
55
54
North Channel
Rathlin I.
Fair Hd
Ballycastle
Malin Hd
Lough Swilly
Irashbofin
Bloody Foreland
Inch I.
Lough Foyle
Coleraine
Ballykelly
Limavady
Culmore
Londonderry
Scarffhollis
Letterkenny
St Johnstone
LONDONDERRY
R. Bann
ANTRIM
Portglenone
DONEGAL
Boylagh Bay
Lifford
Strabane
Clady
Dungiven Fort
Carrickfergus
Belfast Lough
Bangor
Newtown Ards
Donegal
TYRONE
Lough Neagh
Belfast
ULSTER
Omagh
Donaghmore
Dungannon
Donegal Bay
Bundrowes
Ballyshannon
R. Erne
Lough Erne
Belleek
Trillick
Benburb
Charlemont
Moira
Dromore
Killyleagh
Hillsborough
Portmore
Lisburn
DOWN
L. Strangford
L. Melvin
FERMANAGH
Portadown
Armagh
Downpatrick
Killala Bay
Sligo Bay
Sligo
Enniskillen
Lisnaskea
Upper Lough Erne
Monaghan
ARMAGH
Erris Hd
Killala
Dromahaire
Clones
Newtown Butler
MONAGHAN
Moyry Pass
Newry
Dundrum B.
SLIGO
New Town
Belturbet
Castle Blaney
R. Fane
Carlingford
Greencastle
Carlingford Lough
Blacksod Bay
Lough Conn
Curlew Hills
CAVAN
Jamestown
Lough Oughter
Cavan
Dundalk
Dundalk Bay
Achill I.
MAYO
Boyle
Elphin
Virginia
R. Dee
Ardee
Clew Bay
ROSCOMMON
Tulsk
LONGFORD
Longford
Mellifont Abbey
Slane
Beaulieu
Drogheda
CONNAUGHT
Kells
MEATH
Navan
Duleek
Naul
Skerries
Ardmore
Castlecoote
Roscommon
Athboy
Rathconnell
Ardsallagh
Portlester
Lough Mask
Tuam
R. Clare
Lough Ree
Mullingar
WESTMEATH
Trim
Tecroghan
Ballymore
Kinnegad
Moyvally
Slyne Hd
OCEAN

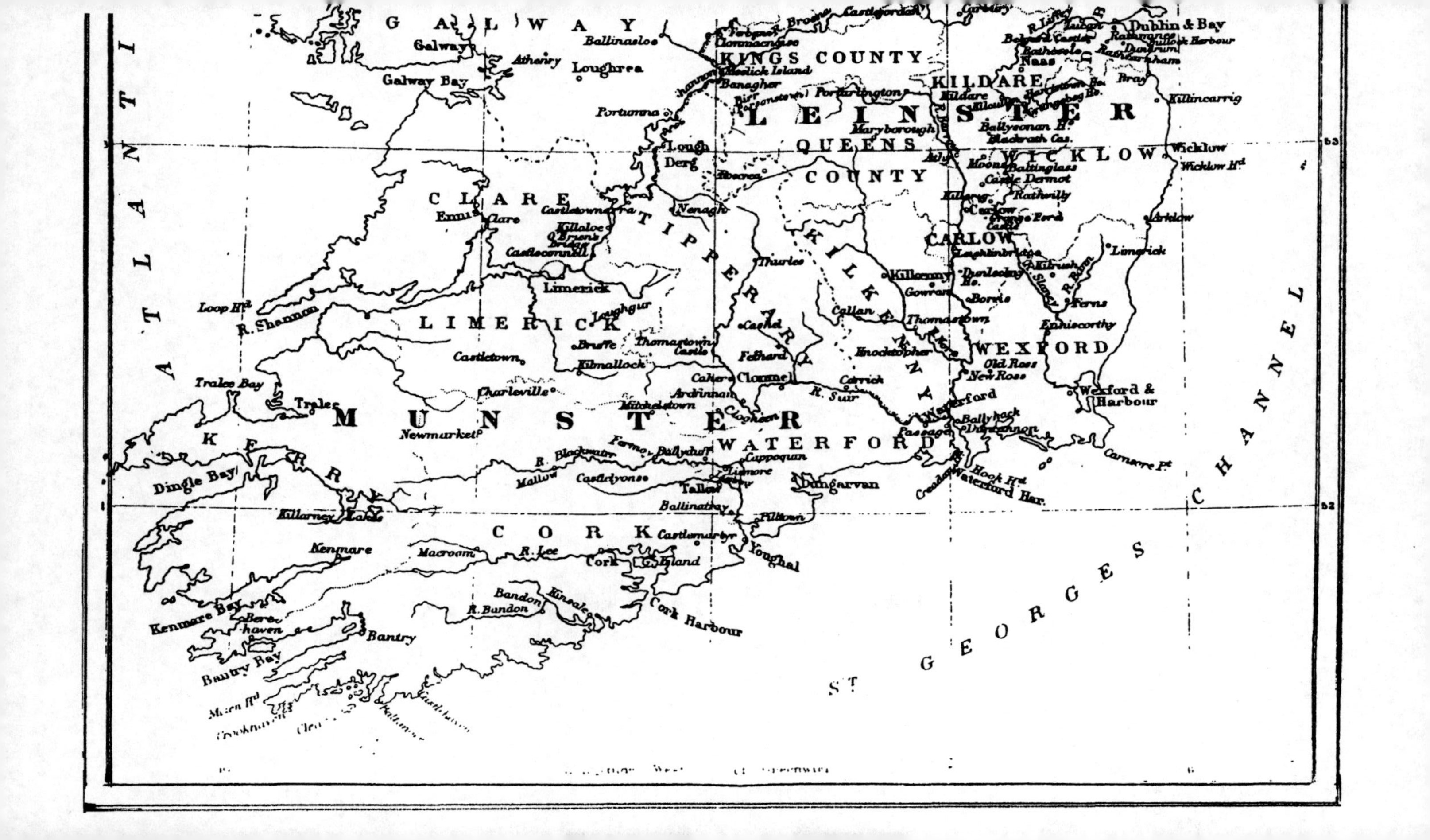

ATLANTIC
GALWAY
Galway
Galway Bay
Atheiry
Loughrea
Ballinasloe
Portumna
KINGS COUNTY
Banagher
Portarlington
KILDARE
Kildare
Naas
Dublin & Bay
Bray
Killincarrig
LEINSTER
Maryborough
QUEENS COUNTY
WICKLOW
Wicklow
Wicklow Hd
Baltinglass
Castle Dermot
Rathvilly
Arklow
CARLOW
Carlow
Limerick
Lough Derg
Roscrea
Nenagh
CLARE
Ennis
Clare
Killaloe
Castleconnell
TIPPERARY
Thurles
KILKENNY
Killenny
Gowran
Borris
Ferns
Enniscorthy
Callan
Thomastown
WEXFORD
Old Ross
New Ross
Wexford & Harbour
Loop Hd
R. Shannon
Limerick
LIMERICK
Castletown
Kilmallock
Cashel
Fethard
Knocktopher
Clonmell
Carrick
R. Suir
Waterford
Charleville
Tralee Bay
Tralee
Mitchelstown
MUNSTER
Newmarket
Ballyhack
Passage
WATERFORD
Cappoquin
Carnsore Pt
KERRY
Dingle Bay
R. Blackwater
Mallow
Castlelyons
Lismore
Dungarvan
Hook Hd
Waterford Har.
Tallow
Ballinatray
Killarney Lakes
CORK
Castlemartyr
Youghal
Kenmare
Macroom
R. Lee
Cork
Island
Bandon
Kinsale
R. Bandon
Cork Harbour
Kenmare Bay
Berehaven
Bantry
Bantry Bay
ST GEORGES CHANEL
53
52

IRISH EMIGRANTS

IN

NORTH AMERICA

ADAM, WILLIAM, and family, emigrated from Belfast on the St James, Captain Mark Collin, landed in Newcastle, Delaware, 22.7.1789. [Pa.Pkt.27.7.1789]

ADAMS, WILLIAM, with his wife, 2 sons and 3 daughters, emigrated from Ireland to Canada on the Alexander 20.6.1815, settled in Bathurst 24.9.1815. [PAO]

AGNEW, ALEXANDER, emigrated from Belfast on the St James, Captain Mark Collin, landed in Newcastle, Delaware, 22.7.1789. [Pa.Pkt.27.7.1789]

AITON, JOSEPH, with his wife, son and 3 daughters, emigrated from Ireland to Canada on the General Moore 8.8.1817, settled in Landsdowne 21.10.1817. [PAO]

ALLEMACE, GEORGE, emigrated from Ireland to Canada on the Mary and Betty 6.1819, settled in Bathurst 6.1820. [PAO]

ANDERSON, ABRAHAM, emigrated from Londonderry on the Nancy of Londonderry, master Thomas Crawford, landed at Newcastle, Delaware, 3.9.1789. [Pa.Pkt.7.9.1789]

ARMOUR, JOHN, son of William Armour in Kilcliff parish, County Down, graduated MA from Glasgow University 1747, settled in Virginia by 1750. [GG]

ARMSTRONG, G., emigrated from Londonderry on the Nancy of Londonderry, master Thomas Crawford, landed at Newcastle, Delaware, 3.9.1789. [Pa.Pkt.7.9.1789]

ARMSTRONG, JOHN, and wife, emigrated from Belfast on the St James, Captain Mark Collin, landed in Newcastle, Delaware, 22.7.1789. [Pa.Pkt.27.7.1789]

ATKINS, SAMUEL, and his wife, emigrated from Ireland to Canada on the Mary Ann 1.8.1817, settled in Elizabethtown 20.9.1817. [PAO]

ATKINS, WALTER, with his wife and 2 sons, emigrated from Ireland to Canada on the Mary Ann 1.8.1817, settled in Elizabethtown 20.9.1817. [PAO]

ATKINSON, JOHN, emigrated from Londonderry on the Ann of Londonderry, master James Ramage, landed in Philadelphia 2.12.1785. [Pa.Pkt.6.12.1785]

BAIRD, JOHN, emigrated from Londonderry on the Ann of Londonderry, master James Ramage, landed in Philadelphia 2.12.1785. [Pa.Pkt.6.12.1785]

BALIN, HUGH, a laborer, born in Ireland 1796, arrived in Richmond on the schooner Emerald late 1821. [USNA]

BALL, ARCHIBALD, and wife, emigrated from Belfast on the St James, Captain Mark Collin, landed in Newcastle, Delaware, 22.7.1789. [Pa.Pkt.27.7.1789]

BARCLAY, JOHN, emigrated from Belfast on the St James, Captain Mark Collin, landed in Newcastle, Delaware, 22.7.1789. [Pa.Pkt.27.7.1789]

BARRINGTON, JAMES, and his wife, emigrated from Ireland to Canada on the General Moore 8.8.1817, settled in Landsdowne 21.10.1817. [PAO]

BARRON, JOHN, and family, emigrated from Belfast on the St James, Captain Mark Collin, landed in Newcastle, Delaware, 27.7.1789. [Pa.Pkt.27.7.1789]

BEATTY, PATRICK, emigrated from Belfast on the St James, Captain Mark Collin, landed in Newcastle, Delaware, 22.7.1789. [Pa.Pkt.27.7.1789]

BELL, DAVID, and family, emigrated from Belfast on the St James, Captain Mark Collin, landed in Newcastle, Delaware, 22.7.1789. [Pa.Pkt.27.7.1789]

BELL, JAMES, emigrated from Ireland to Canada on the Suffolk, 8.6.1820, settled in Bathurst 7.9.1820. [PAO]

BELL, ROBERT, and family, emigrated from Belfast on the St James, Captain Mark Collin, landed in Newcastle, Delaware, 22.7.1789. [Pa.Pkt.27.7.1789]

BELL, ROBERT, emigrated from Belfast on the St James, Captain Mark Collin, landed in Newcastle, Delaware, 22.7.1789. [Pa.Pkt.27.7.1789]

BEVEARD, JOHN, emigrated from Londonderry on the Ann of Londonderry, master James Ramage, landed in Philadelphia 2.12.1785. [Pa.Pkt.6.12.1785]

BIGGINS, JAMES, and wife, emigrated from Ireland to Canada on the Atlantic, arrived 14.8.1817, settled in Kitley 27.3.1818. [PAO]

BIGGS, ALEXANDER, emigrated from Ireland to Canada on the Sophia 9.6.1820, settled in Drummond 2.9.1820. [PAO]

BIGNEL, JAMES, with his wife and 2 sons, emigrated from Ireland to Canada on the Mary and Betty 1816, settled in Landsdowne 29.11.1817. [PAO]

BOOMER, RAINEY, emigrated from Belfast on the St James, Captain Mark Collin, landed in Newcastle, Delaware, 22.7.1789. [Pa.Pkt.27.7.1789]

BOULTON, RICHARD, emigrated from Ireland to Canada on the Mary Ann 19.8.1817, settled in Oxford 8.10.1817. [PAO]

BOYD, JAMES, emigrated from Belfast on the St James, landed in Newcastle, Delaware, 22.7.1789. [Pa.Pkt.27.7.1789]

BOYD, JOHN, emigrated from Belfast on the St James, Captain Mark Collin, landed in Newcastle, Delaware, 22.7.1789. [Pa.Pkt.27.7.1789]

BOYD, WILLIAM, emigrated from Londonderry on the Nancy of Londonderry, master Thomas Crawford, landed at Newcastle, Delaware, 3.9.1789. [Pa.Pkt.7.9.1789]

BOYLE, CHARLES, emigrated from Londonderry on the brig Mary of Londonderry, Captain Cassidy, landed at Philadelphia 12.1789. [P.M.5.12.1789]

BOYLE, SAMUEL, and his wife, emigrated from Ireland to Canada on the Mary and Ann 4.8.1817, settled in Marlborough 4.11.1817. [PAO]

BRADLEY, JOHN, with his wife and 3 daughters, emigrated from Ireland to Canada on the Mary and Ann 4.8.1817, settled in Oxford 30.11.1817. [PAO]

BRADLEY, SAMUEL, with his wife, 5 sons and 1 daughter, emigrated from Ireland to Canada on the Mary and Ann 4.8.1817, settled in Oxford 30.11.1817. [PAO]

BRADLEY, WILLIAM, a laborer, born in Ireland 1799, arrived in Richmond on the schooner Emerald late 1821. [USNA]

BRIGGS, THOMAS, emigrated from Ireland to Canada on the Columbia 7.1819, settled in Bathurst 20.2.1821. [PAO]

BROWN, DAVID, emigrated from Londonderry on the Ann of Londonderry, master James Ramage, landed in Philadelphia 2.12.1785. [Pa.Pkt.6.12.1785]

BROWN, JAMES, emigrated from Londonderry on the Ann of Londonderry, master James Ramage, landed in Philadelphia 2.12.1785. [Pa.Pkt.6.12.1785]

BROWN, JAMES, emigrated from Belfast on the St James, Captain Mark Collin, landed in Newcastle, Delaware, 22.7.1789. [Pa.Pkt.27.7.1789]

BROWNE, JAMES, emigrated from Londonderry on the brig Conyngham, master Robert Conyngham, landed in Newcastle, Delaware, 7.1789. [P.M.11.8.1789]

BROWN, JOHN, emigrated from Londonderry on the Ann of Londonderry, master James Ramage, landed in Philadelphia 2.12.1785. [Pa.Pkt.6.12.1785]

BROWN, JOHN, and family, emigrated from Belfast on the St James, Captain Mark Collin, landed in Newcastle, Delaware, 22.7.1789. [Pa.Pkt.27.7.1789]

BROWN, SAMUEL, and wife, emigrated from Belfast on the St James, Captain Mark Collin, landed in Newcastle, Delaware, 22.7.1789. [Pa.Pkt.27.71789]

BRYAN, WILLIAM, with his wife, a son and 2 daughters, emigrated from Ireland to Canada on the Atlantic 27.6.1819, settled in Bathurst 8.1820. [PAO]

BURNES, LAURENCE, emigrated from Ireland to Canada 15.5.1820, settled in Drummond 5.9.1820. [PAO]

BURNS, BERNARD, emigrated from Belfast on the St James, Captain Mark Collin, landed in Newcastle, Delaware, 22.7.1789. [Pa.Pkt.27.7.1789]

CAMMEL, JOHN, a laborer, born 1767, Margaret born 1797, Catherine born 1767, Agnes born 1802, Cornelius, a laborer, born 1799, Mary Ann born 1798, John born 1806, and Thomas, a laborer, born 1808, all born in Ireland, arrived in Alexandria late 1821 on the schooner Thetis, Captain Newcombe. [USNA]

CAMMEL, MARY, born 1765, with children, all born in Ireland, arrived in Alexandria late 1821 on the schooner Thetis, Captain Newcombe. [USNA]

CAMPBELL, JOHN, emigrated from Londonderry on the Ann of Londonderry, master James Ramage, landed in Philadelphia 2.12.1785. [Pa.Pkt.6.12.1785]

CARLISLE. ANDREW, emigrated from Londonderry on the brig Conyngham, master Robert Conyngham, landed in Newcastle, Delaware, 7.1789. [P.M.11.8.1789]

CARR, ANDREW, emigrated from Belfast on the St James, Captain Mark Collin, landed in Newcastle, Delaware, 22.7.1789. [Pa.Pkt.27.7.1789]

CARROLL, THOMAS, emigrated from Ireland to Canada on the Pitt 28.7.1820, settled in Bathurst 30.10.1820. [PAO]

CASWELL, ANDREW, emigrated from Ireland to Canada, settled in Drummond 25.8.1820. [PAO]

CAVANAGH, ABRAHAM, with his wife, son and 2 daughters, emigrated from Ireland to Canada on the Mary and Bell 23.8.1817, settled in Yonge 21.10.1817. [PAO]

CAVANAGH, JOHN, emigrated from Ireland to Canada on the Active 7.1818, settled in Beckwith 1818. [PAO]

CHANNING, JOHN, with his wife and 2 daughters, emigrated from Ireland to Canada, settled in Lancaster 3.12.1821. [PAO]

CHRISTY, DANIEL, emigrated from Londonderry on the Ann of Londonderry, master James Ramage, landed in Philadelphia 2.12.1785. [Pa.Pkt.6.12.1785]

CLAICKS, JOHN, emigrated from Ireland to Canada, settled in Bathurst 2.9.1820. [PAO]

CLARKE, JAMES, emigrated from Belfast on the St James, Captain Mark Collin, landed in Newcastle, Delaware, 22.7.1789. [Pa.Pkt.27.7.1789]

CLEMENS, DAVID, emigrated from Newry on the brig Havannah, Captain Sutter, landed in Philadelphia 1.8.1789. [Pa.Pkt.6.8.1789]

COCHRANE, ALEXANDER, and family, emigrated from Belfast on the St James, Captain Mark Collin, landed in Newcastle, Delaware, 22.7.1789. [Pa.Pkt.27.7.1789]

COCHRAN, JOHN, emigrated from Newry on the brig Havannah, Captain Sutter, landed in Philadelphia 1.8.1789. [Pa.Pkt.6.8.1789]

CODD, GEORGE, emigrated from Ireland to Canada, settled in Lancaster 11.11.1821. [PAO]

CODD, JOHN, with his wife, son and 2 daughters, emigrated from Ireland to Canada on the John 19.9.1815, settled in Drummond 11.11.1815. [PAO]

CODD, THOMAS, with his wife and 5 sons, emigrated from Ireland to Canada, settled in Lancaster 10.11.1821. [PAO]

COLBURN, WILLIAM, with his wife and a daughter, emigrated from Ireland to Canada on the General Moore 20.8.1817, settled in Oxford 12.1.1818. [PAO]

COLLINS, EDWARD, emigrated from Londonderry on the Nancy of Londonderry, Captain Cassidy, landed in Philadelphia 12.1789. [P.M.5.12.1789]

CONNOR, JOHN, with his wife, son and daughter, emigrated from Ireland to Canada on the John 19.9.1815, settled in Drummond 20.11.1815. [PAO]

CONNORS, THOMAS, with wife, son and two daughters, to Canada on the Atlantic, arrived 14.8.1817, settled in Kitley 27.3.1818. [PAO]

CONROY, EDWARD, emigrated from Newry on the brig Havannah, Captain Sutter, landed in Philadelphia 1.8.1789. [Pa.Pkt.6.8.1789]

COPELAND, BENJAMIN, with his wife and daughter, emigrated from Ireland to Canada on the Mary and Ann 4.8.1817, settled in Marlborough 4.11.1817. [PAO]

COX, JOHN, with his wife and 2 daughters, to Canada on the Maria, arrived 5.8.1817, settled in Yonge 14.3.1818.[PAO]

CRAIG, SAMUEL, Derry, emigrated from Ireland to Canada on the Alexander 20.6.1815, settled in Drummond 19.7.1815. [PAO]

CRAWFORD, WALLIS, emigrated from Londonderry on the Ann of Londonderry, master James Ramage, landed in Philadelphia 2.12.1785. [Pa.Pkt.6.12.1785]

CROSKREY, WILLIAM, with his wife and daughter, emigrated from Ireland to Canada on the Rodney 4.6.1820, settled in Drummond 5.9.1820. [PAO]

CUNNINGHAM, ROBERT, emigrated from Londonderry on the Nancy of Londonderry, master Thomas Crawford, landed at Newcastle, Delaware, 3.9.1789. [Pa.Pkt.7.9.1789]

CUNNINGHAM, WILLIAM, emigrated from Newry on the brig Havanna, Captain Sutter landed in Philadelphia 1.8.1789. [Pa.Pkt.6.8.1789]

CURRIE, JOHN, with his wife and daughter, County Tyrone, emigrated from Ireland to Canada on the Alexander, 20.6.1815, settled in Bathurst 19.7.1815. [PAO]

DALZELL, JANE, and family, emigrated from Belfast on the St James, Captain Mark Collin, landed in Newcastle, Delaware, 22.7.1789. [Pa.Pkt.27.7.1789]

DAVELIN, SALLY, born in Ireland 1795, arrived in Richmond on the schooner Emerald late 1821. [USNA]

DAVIES, EDWARD, and his wife, emigrated from Ireland to Canada on the Betty and Mary, 8.1.1818, settled in South Crosby 4.1.1818. [PAO]

DEACON, JAMES, sr., with his wife, 3 sons and 2 daughters, emigrated from Ireland to Canada on the Commerce 19.9.1815, settled in Drummond 18.10.1815. [PAO]

DEACON, JAMES, jr., with his wife, son and daughter, emigrated fron Ireland to Canada on the John 19.9.1815, settled in Drummond 19.11.1815. [PAO]

DEACON, MICHAEL, emigrated from Ireland to Canada on the Saltham 1.8.1817, settled in South Gower 25.11.1817. [PAO]

DENES, HUGH, emigrated from Londonderry on the Nancy of Londonderry, master Thomas Crawford, landed at Newcastle, Delaware, 3.9.1789. [Pa.Pkt.7.9.1789]

DENNAM, WILLIAM, emigrated from Belfast on the St James, Captain Mark Collin, landed in Newcastle, Delaware, 22.7.1789. [Pa.Pkt.27.7.1789]

DENNY, JANE, born in Donegal 1753, settled in Londonderry, Colchester County, Nova Scotia, by 1761, wife of Robert Dill. [Folly Village g/s, N.S.]

DERBY, KITTY, born in Ireland 1792, arrived in Alexandria late 1821 on the schooner Southern Trader, Captain Simpson. [USNA]

DICKY, ABRAHAM, County Antrim, emigrated from Ireland to Canada on the Alexander 20.6.1815, settled in Drummond 19.7.1815. [PAO]

DILL, ROBERT, born in Donegal, 1740, settled in Londonderry, Colchester County, Nova Scotia, by 1761. [Folly Village g/s, N.S.]

DIVER, JAMES, a laborer, born in Ireland 1803, arrived in Richmond on the schooner Emerald late 1821. [USNA]

DORRES, JAMES, emigrated from Newry on the brig Havannah, Captain Sutter, landed in Philadelphia 1.8.1789. [Pa.Pkt.6.8.1789]

DOUGLAS, JOHN, emigrated from Londonderry on the Nancy of Londonderry. master Thomas Crawford, landed at Newcastle, Delaware, 3.9.1789. [Pa.Pkt.7.9.1789]

DOW, JOHN, emigrated from Ireland to Canada on the Mary and Betty 6.1819, settled in Sherbrooke 6.1820. [PAO]

DOWSLEY, THOMAS, emigrated from Ireland to Canada on the Mary and Betty 6.1819, settled in Sherbrooke 6.1820. [PAO]

DOYLE, SAMUEL, emigrated from Ireland to Canada on the Atlantic 14.8.1817, settled in Oxford 9.12.1817. [PAO]

DROUPE, WILLIAM, with his wife, a son and 2 daughters, emigrated from Ireland to Canada on the Atlantic 7.1820, settled in Bathurst 28.10.1820. [PAO]

DUCANNY, JOHN, emigrated from Londonderry on the Ann of Londonderry, master James Ramage, 2.12.1785. [Pa.Pkt.6.12.1785]

DUFFY, PIERCE, emigrated from Belfast on the St James, Captain Mark Collin, landed in Newcastle, Delaware, 22.7.1789. [Pa.Pkt.27.7.1789]

DUNEGAN, JOHN, emigrated from Newry on the brig Havannah, Captain Sutter, landed in Philadelphia 1.8.1789. [Pa.Pkt.6.8.1789]

DUNLAP, ROBERT, and family, emigrated from Belfast on the St James, Captain Mark Collin, landed in Newcastle, Delaware, 22.7.1789. [Pa.Pkt.27.7.1789]

DUNSMOOR, JOHN, emigrated from Newry on the brig Havannah, Captain Sutter, landed in Philadelphia 1.8.1789. [Pa.Pkt.6.8.1789]

ELLIOT, JAMES, emigrated from Londonderry on the Nancy of Londonderry, master Thomas Crawford, landed at Newcastle, Delaware, 3.9.1789. [Pa.Pkt.7.9.1789]

ELLIS, GEORGE, emigrated from Londonderry on the Ann of Londonderry, master James Ramage, landed in Philadelphia 2.12.1785. [Pa.Pkt.6.12.1785]

EVETT, HENRY, and 2 daughters, emigrated from Ireland to Canada on the Swansea 11.1817, settled in Yonge 14.2.1818. [PAO]

EWART, JOHN, emigrated from Newry on the brig Havannah, Captain Sutter, landed in Philadelphia 1.8.1789. [Pa.Pkt.6.8.1789]

EWART, JOHN, emigrated from Newry on the brig Havannah, Captain Sutter, landed in Philadelphia 1.8.1789. [Pa.Pkt.6.8.1789]

FAIRLY, HUGH, and family, emigrated from Belfast on the St James, Captain Mark Collin, landed in Newcastle, Delaware, 22.7.1789. [Pa.Pkt.27.7.1789]

FAULKNER, ROBERT, born in Ireland 1733, settled in Folly, Londonderry, Colchester County, Nova Scotia, by 1761. [Folly Village g/s, N.S.]

FERGUSON, ANDREW, emigrated from Belfast on the St James, Captain Mark Collin, landed in Newcastle, Delaware, 22.7.1789. [Pa.Pkt.27.7.1789]

FERGUSON, JAMES, emigrated from Belfast on the St James, Captain Mark Collin, landed in Newcastle, Delaware, 22.7.1789. [Pa.Pkt.27.7.1789]

FINGAY, SAMUEL, and son, emigrated from Belfast on the St James, Captain Mark Collin, landed in Newcastle, Delaware, 22.7.1789. [Pa.Pkt.27.7.1789]

FITZSIMMONS, GEORGE, emigrated from Londonderry on the Ann of Londonderry, master James Ramage, landed in Philadelphia 2.12.1785. [Pa.Pkt.6.12.1785]

FLEMMING, JAMES, born in Londonderry, Ireland, 1741, settled in Folly, Londonderry, Colchester County, Nova Scotia, by 1761, husband of Isabella born 1750. [Folly Village g/s, N.S.]

FLETCHER, THOMAS, born in Ireland 1738, settled in Folly, Londonderry, Colchester County, Nova Scotia, by 1761, husband of Jane Vance born in Ireland 1753. [Folly Village g/s, N.S.]

FLETCHER, WILLIAM, born 1725, and his wife Elenor born 1740, settled in Londonderry, Colchester County, Nova Scotia, by 1761. [Folly Village g/s. N.S.]

FLINN, JOHN, emigrated from Ireland to Canada, settled in Lancaster 11.11.1821. [PAO]

FLOOD, JOHN, with his wife, 2 sons and 1 daughter, emigrated from Ireland to Canada on the Marmion 8.1819, settled in Bathurst 20.2.1820. [PAO]

FLOOD, OWEN, emigrated from Ireland to Canada, settled in Dalhousie 7.11.1821. [PAO]

FULLEN, THOMAS, with his wife, son and daughter, County Tyrone, emigrated from Ireland to Canada on the Alexander 20.6.1815, settled in Bathurst 19.7.1815. [PAO]

GALLEY, EDWARD, emigrated from Newry on the brig Havannah, Captain Sutter, landed in Philadelphia 1.8.1789. [Pa.Pkt.6.8.1789]

GEARY, WILLIAM, emigrated from Newry on the brig Havannah, Captain Sutter, landed in Philadelphia 1.8.1789. [Pa.Pkt.6.8.1789]

GEARY, WILLIAM, emigrated from Newry on the brig Havannah, landed in Philadelphia 1.8.1789. [Pa.Pkt.6.8.1789]

GEE, Mr M., born in Ireland 1797, arrived in Alexandria on the ship Boston, Captain Fenly, late 1821. [USNA]

GIBBON, JOHN, born 1799 in Ireland, a laborer, arrived in Richmond on the schooner Emerald late 1821. [USNA]

GILLESPIE, FRANCIS, emigrated from Ireland to Canada on the Isabella 26.6.1820, settled in Bathurst 12.1820. [PAO]

GILMOUR, THOMAS, emigrated from Londonderry on the Ann of Londonderry, master James Ramage, landed in Philadelphia 2.12.1785. [Pa.Pkt.6.12.1785]

GIPSON, JOHN, emigrated from Londonderry on the Ann of Londonderry, master James Hewitt, landed in Philadelphia 2.12.1785. [Pa.Pkt.6.12.1785]

GLASS, ISAAC, and family, emigrated from Belfast on the St James, Captain Mark Collin, landed in Newcastle, Delaware, 22.7.1789. [Pa.Pkt.27.7.1789]

GODKIN, THOMAS, to Canada on the Mary and Bell, arrived 9.7.1817, settled in South Crosby 30.3.1818.[PAO]

GODKIN, THOMAS, emigrated from Ireland to Canada on the Mary and Bell 4.8.1817, settled in South Gower 25.11.1817. [PAO]

GORDON, ALEXANDER, emigrated from Belfast on the St James, Captain Mark Collin, landed in Newcastle, Delaware, 22.7.1789. [Pa.Pkt.27.7.1789]

GORDON, WILLIAM, emigrated from Belfast on the St James, Captain Mark Collin, landed in Newcastle, Delaware, 22.7.1789. [Pa.Pkt.27.7.1789]

GRAHAM, WILLIAM, with his wife and 2 daughters, emigrated from Ireland to Canada on the Active 9.8.1817, settled in Yonge Escott 17.1.1818. [PAO]

GRAHMS, DANIEL, emigrated from Londonderry on the Ann of Londonderry, master James Ramage, landed in Philadelphia 2.12.1785. [Pa.Pkt.6.12.1785]

GRAY, HUGH, emigrated from Londonderry on the Nancy of Londonderry, master Thomas Crawford, landed at Newcastle, Delaware, 3.9.1789. [Pa.Pkt.7.9.1789]

GRAY, ROBERT, jr., emigrated from Londonderry on the Ann of Londonderry, master James Ramage, landed in Philadelphia 2.12.1785. [Pa.Pkt.6.12.1785]

GREEN, SAMUEL, with wife, son, and two daughters, to Canada on the Mary and Bell, arrived 9.7.1817, settled in Lansdowne 31.3.1818.[PAO]

HAGOWAN, ALEXANDER, emigrated from Belfast on the St James, Captain Mark Collin, landed in Newcastle, Delaware, 22.7.1789. [Pa.Pkt.27.7.1789]

HAMILTON, JAMES, and sister, emigrated from Belfast on the St James, Captain Mark Collin, landed in Newcastle, Delaware, 22.7.1789. [Pa.Pkt.27.7.1789]

HAMILTON, RICHARD, emigrated from Londonderry on the brig Mary of Londonderry, Captain Cassidy, landed in Philadelphia 12.1789. [P.M.5.12.1789]

HAMILTON, ROBERT, with his wife and 5 sons, emigrated from Ireland to Canada on the Eliza 14.5.1820, settled in Bathurst 16.2.1821. [PAO]

HAMILTON, WILLIAM, emigrated from Ireland to Canada on the Hariot 28.6.1815, settled in Bathurst 14.10.1815. [PAO]

HANEY, JANE, emigrated from Belfast on the St James, Captain Mark Collin, landed in Newcastle, Delaware, 22.7.1789. [Pa.Pkt.27.7.1789]

HANNA, ABRAHAM, emigrated from Newry on the brig Havannah, Captain Sutter, landed in Philadelphia 1.8.1789. [Pa.Pkt.6.8.1789]

HARBISON, SAMUEL, and family, emigrated from Belfast on the St James, landed in Newcastle, Delaware, 22.7.1789. [Pa.Pkt.27.7.1789]

HARDY, THOMAS, emigrated from Londonderry on the brig Conyngham, landed in Newcastle, Delaware, 7.1789. [P.M.11.8.1789]

HARRIS, JAMES, and family, emigrated from Belfast on the St James, Captain Mark Collin, landed in Newcastle, Delaware, 22.7.1789. [Pa.Pkt.27.7.1789]

HARVEY, SAMUEL, emigrated from Newry on the brig Havannah, Captain Sutter, landed in Philadelphia 1.8.1789. [Pa.Pkt.6.8.1780]

HAYSE, JOHN, emigrated from Belfast on the St James, Captain Mark Collin, landed in Newcastle, Delaware, 22.7.1789. [Pa.Pkt.27.7.1789]

HENDERSON, R., a farmer, born in Ireland 1771, with wife Mary born in Ireland 1783, and their five children, arrived in Richmond late 1821 on the schooner Emerald. [USNA]

HENDERSON, WILLIAM, a weaver, born in Ireland 1775, with wife Martha born in Ireland 1777 and 5 children, arrived in Richmond on the schooner Emerald late 1821. [USNA]

HENRY, JOSEPH, emigrated from Belfast on the St James, Captain Mark Collin, landed in Newcastle, Delaware, 22.7.1789. [Pa.Pkt.27.7.1789]

HENRY, WILLIAM, and family, emigrated from Belfast on the St James, Captain Mark Collin, landed in Newcastle, Delaware, 22.7.1789. [Pa.Pkt.27.7.1789]

HESLIP, JAMES, emigrated from Newry on the brig Havannah, Captain Sutter, landed in Philadelphia 1.8.1789. [Pa.Pkt.6.8.1789]

HEWITT, THOMAS, emigrated from Londonderry on the Ann of Londonderry, master James Ramage, landed in Philadelphia 2.12.1785. [Pa.Pkt.6.12.1785]

HIDDLESTON, ROBERT, with his wife and son, emigrated from Ireland to Canada on the Suffolk 8.6.1820, settled in Bathurst 4.9.1820. [PAO]

HIGGINS, EDWARD, emigrated from Ireland to Canada, settled in Drummond 11.2.1821. [PAO]

HILL, CHARLES, emigrated from Londonderry on the Nancy of Londonderry, Captain Cassidy, landed in Philadelphia 12.1789. [P.M.5.12.1789]

HILL, WILLIAM, emigrated from Londonderry on the Nancy of Londonderry, Captain Cassidy, landed in Philadelphia 12.1789. [P.M.5.12.1789]

HOLLIDAY, WILLIAM, and family, emigrated from Belfast on the St James, landed in Newcastle, Delaware, 22.7.1789. [Pa.Pkt.27.7.1789]

HORON, JOHN, emigrated from Belfast on the St James, Captain Mark Collin, landed in Newcastle, Delaware, 22.7.1789. [Pa.Pkt.27.7.1789]

HUGHES, OWEN, and his wife, emigrated from Ireland to Canada, settled in Dalhousie 7.11.1821. [PAO]

HUMPHRIES, JAMES, emigrated from Londonderry on the brig Conyngham, naster Robert Conyngham, landed in Newcastle, Delaware, 7.1789. [P.M.11.8.1789]

HUMPHREYS, WILLIAM, emigrated from Londonderry on the Ann of Londonderry, master James Ramage, landed in Philadelphia 2.12.1785. [Pa.Pkt.6.12.1785]

INGRAM, WILLIAM, emigrated from Newry on the brig Havannah, Captain Sutter, landed in Philadelphia 1.8.1789. [Pa.Pkt.6.8.1789]

IRVINE, WILLIAM, emigrated from Londonderry on the Ann of Londonderry, master James Ramage, landed in Philadelphia 2.12.1785. [Pa.Pkt.6.12.1785]

IRWIN, SAMUEL, emigrated from Belfast on the St James, Captain Mark Collin, landed in Newcastle, Delaware, 22.7.1789. [Pa.Pkt.27.7.1789]

JACKMAN, JOHN, emigrated from Ireland to Canada on the Ann 20.7.1820, settled in Bathurst 6.11.1820. [PAO]

JAMES, JOHN, emigrated from Ireland {via New York?} to Canada on the brig Charles Miller 19.9.1815, settled in Drummond 6.11.1815. [PAO]

JAMES, JOHN, emigrated from Ireland to Canada, settled in Lancaster 9.11.1821. [PAO]

JAMES, JOSEPH, emigrated from Ireland to Canada, settled in Lancaster 9.11.1821. [PAO]

JAMES, THOMAS, with his wife, emigrated from Ireland {via New York?} to Canada on the brig Charles Miller 19.9.1815, settled in Drummond 6.11.1815. [PAO]

JAMES, WILLIAM, emigrated fron Ireland {via New York?} to Canada on the brig Charles Miller 19.9.1815, settled in Drummond 16.11.1815. [PAO]

JAMES, WILLIAM, sr., with his wife and son, emigrated from Ireland to Canada, settled in Lancaster 9.11.1821. [PAO]

JAMES, WILLIAM, emigrated from Ireland to Canada, settled in Lancaster 9.11.1821. [PAO]

JARDAINE, THOMAS, emigrated from Belfast on the St James, Captain Mark Collin, landed in Newcastle, Delaware, 22.7.1789. [Pa.Pkt.27.7.1789]

JOHNSON, ABRAHAM, with his wife, a son and a daughter, emigrated from Ireland to Canada on the Atlantic 7.1820, settled in Bathurst 28.10.1820. [PAO]

JOHNSON, RICHARD, emigrated from Londonderry on the Nancy of Londonderry, master Thomas Crawford, landed at Newcastle, Delaware, 3.9.1789. [Pa.Pkt.7.9.1789]

JOHNSTON, EDWARD, with his wife and 2 daughters, emigrated from Ireland to Canada on the Atlantic 22.6.1819, settled in Bathurst 23.1.1821. [PAO]

JOHNSTON, GEORGE, and his wife, emigrated from Ireland to Canada on the Virginia 30.9.1817, settled in Landsdowne 23.12.1817. [PAO]

JOHNSTON, GEORGE, and wife, to Canada, arrived 14.7.1817, settled in Leeds 28.3.1818.[PAO]

JOHNSTON, HENRY, with his wife, a son and 3 daughters, emigrated from Ireland to Canada on the Virginia 30.9.1817, settled in Landsdowne 23.12.1817. [PAO]

JOHNSTON, HUGH, emigrated from Belfast on the St James, Captain Mark Collin, landed in Newcastle, Delaware, 22.7.1789. [Pa.Pkt.27.7.1789]

JOHNSTON, WILLIAM, emigrated from Londonderry on the Ann of Londonderry, master James Ramage, landed in Philadelphia 2.12.1785. [Pa.Pkt.6.12.1785]

KELLEY, ANDREW, emigrated from Newry on the brig Havannah, Captain Sutter, landed in Philadelphia 1.8.1789. [Pa.Pkt.6.8.1789]

KELLY, JOHN, emigrated from Ireland to Canada on the Eolus 5.1820, settled in Drummond 8.12.1820. [PAO]

KELLY, THOMAS, and his wife, emigrated from Ireland to Canada on the John 19.9.1815, settled in Drummond 11.11.1815. [PAO]

KELSO, HUGH, emigrated from Londonderry on the Nancy of Londonderry, Captain Cassidy, landed at Philadelphia 12.1789. [P.M.5.12.1789]

KENNEDY, ARCHIBALD, County Antrim, emigrated from Ireland to Canada on the Alexander 20.6.1815, settled in Drummond 19.7.1815. [PAO]

KENNY, JAMES, emigrated from Ireland to Canada, settled in Lancaster 7.11.1821. [PAO]

KENNY, WILLIAM, emigrated from Ireland to Canada, settled in Dalhousie 7.11.1821. [PAO]

KERR, JOHN, emigrated from Newry on the brig Havannah, Captain Sutter, landed in Philadelphia 1.8.1789. [Pa.Pkt.6.8.1789]

KING, JOSEPH, with his wife and 2 sons, County Armagh, emigrated from Ireland to Canada on the Alexander 20.6.1815, settled in Bathurst 19.7.1815. [PAO]

KINNY, JAMES, with wife, two sons and two daughters, to Canada on the Loyal Samuel, arrived 25.8.1817, settled in Landsdowne 19.3.1818.[PAO]

KIRKWOOD, THOMAS, emigrated from Londonderry on the brig Conyngham, master Robert Conyngham, landed in Newcastle, Delaware, 7.1789. [P.M.11.8.1789]

KYLE, JEREMIAH, emigrated from Londonderry on the Nancy of Londonderry, master Thomas Crawfordm landed at Newcastle, Delaware, 3.9.1789. [Pa.Pkt.7.9.1789]

LAMBERT, JOHN, emigrated from Ireland to Canada on the Mary and Betty, 6.1819, settled in Bathurst 1.10.1820. [PAO]

LAW, ROBERT, and family, emigrated from Belfast on the St James, Captain Mark Collin, landed in Newcastle, Delaware, 22.7.1789. [Pa.Pkt.27.7.1789]

LEANEY, JOSEPH, emigrated from Londonderry on the Ann of Londonderry, master James Ramage, landed in Philadelphia 2.12.1785. [Pa.Pkt.6.12.1785]

LEE, WILLIAM, and family, emigrated from Belfast on the St James, Captain Mark Collin, landed in Newcastle, Delaware, 22.7.1789. [Pa.Pkt.27.7.1789]

LEGGETT, JOHN, emigrated from Ireland to Canada on the Atlantic 14.8.1817, settled in South Crosby 19.12.1817. [PAO]

LEGGETT, MARTHA, a widow, with her 4 sons and 1 daughter, emigrated from Ireland to Canada on the Atlantic 14.8.1817, settled in South Crosby 19.12.1817. [PAO]

LEGGETT, ROBERT, emigrated from Ireland to Canada on the Atlantic, 14.8.1817, settled in South Crosby 19.12.1817. [PAO]

LEGGETT, WILLIAM, with his wife, 2 sons and 3 daughters, emigrated from Ireland to Canada on the Atlantic 14.8.1817, settled in South Crosby 19.12.1817. [PAO]

LEMON, JOHN, emigrated from Belfast on the St James, Captain Mark Collin, landed in Newcastle, Delaware, 22.7.1789. [Pa.Pkt.27.7.1789]

LEMON, WILLIAM, emigrated from Belfast on the St James, Captain Mark Collin, landed in Newcastle, Delaware, 22.7.1789. [Pa.Pkt.27.7.1789]

LEYBURN, JOHN, emigrated from Newry on the brig Havannah, Captain Sutter, landed in Philadelphia 1.8.1789. [Pa.Pkt.6.8.1789]

LEYBURN, WILLIAM, emigrated from Newry on the brig Havannah, Captain Sutter, landed in Philadelphia 1.8.1789. [Pa.Pkt.6.8.1789]

LITTLE. PATRICK, County Tyrone, emigrated from Ireland to Canada on the Alexander 20.6.1815, settled in Bathurst 19.7.1815. [PAO]

LORIMER, THOMAS, Belfast, emigrated from Ireland to Canada on the Alexander 20.6.1815, settled in Bathurst 19.7.1815. [PAO]

LOVE, JOHN, emigrated from Newry on the brig Havannah, Captain Sutter, landed in Philadelphia 1.8.1789. [Pa.Pkt.6.8.1789]

LOWRY, JAMES, emigrated from Belfast on the St James, Captain Mark Collin, landed in Newcastle, Delaware, 22.7.1789. [Pa.Pkt.27.7.1789]

LOWRY, JOHN, and family, emigrated from Belfast on the St James, Captain Mark Collin, landed in Newcastle, Delaware, 22.7.1789. [Pa.Pkt.27.7.1789]

LYLE, JOHN, emigrated from Belfast on the St James, Captain Mark Collin, landed in Newcastle, Delaware, 22.7.1789. [Pa.Pkt.27.7.1789]

MCALADE, WILLIAM, emigrated from Belfast on the St James, Captain Mark Collin, landed in Newcastle, Delaware, 22.7.1789. [Pa.Pkt.27.7.1789]

MCAMON, DAVID, emigrated from Newry on the brig Havannah, Captan Sutter, landed in Philadelphia 1.8.1789. [Pa.Pkt.6.8.1789]

MCBLAIR, JAMES, emigrated from Belfast on the St James, Captain Mark Collin, landed in Newcastle, Delaware, 22.7.1789. [Pa.Pkt.27.7.1789]

MCCABE, MICHAEL, with his wife, a son and a daughter, emigrated from Ireland to Canada on the Columbia 4.8.1820, settled in Drummond 18.10.1820. [PAO]

MCCAGHEY. SAMUEL, emigrated from Belfast on the St James, Captain Mark Collin, landed in Newcastle, Delaware. 22.7.1789. [Pa.Pkt.27.7.1789]

MCCAUGHRY, JOHN, emigrated from Belfast on the St James, Captain Mark Collin, landed in Newcastle, Delaware, 22.7.1789. [Pa.Pkt.27.7.1789]

MCCLAY, WILLIAM, emigrated from Ireland to Canada on the Briton 12.1817, settled in Landsdowne 23.12.1817. [PAO]

MCCLONG, WILLIAM, emigrated from Newry on the brig Havannah, Captain Sutter, landed in Philadelphia 1.8.1789. [Pa.Pkt.6.8.1789]

MCCLOUGHAN, JOHN, emigrated from Newry on the brig Havannah, Captain Sutter, landed in Philadelphia 1.8.1789. [Pa.Pkt.6.8.1789]

MCCLUNG, JOSEPH, emigrated from Newry on the brig Havannah, Captain Sutter, landed in Philadelphia 1.8.1789. [Pa.Pkt.6.8.1789]

MCCLUNG, ROBERT, emigrated from Newry on the brig Havannah, Captain Sutter, arrived in Philadelphia 1.8.1789. [Pa.Pkt.6.8.1789]

MCCLUNG, WILLIAM, emigrated from Newry on the brig Havannah, Captain Sutter, landed in Philadelphia 1.8.1789. [Pa.Pkt.6.8.1789]

MCCONE, MATTHEW, emigrated from Newry on the brig Havannah, Captain Sutter, landed in Philadelphia 1.8.1789. [Pa.Pkt.6.8.1789]

MCCONNELL, JOHN, emigrated from Belfast on the St James, Captain Mark Collin, landed in Newcastle, Delaware, 22.7.1789. [Pa.Pkt.27.7.1789]

MCCUE, JAMES, with his wife, a son and 2 daughters, emigrated from Ireland to Canada on the Pitt 28.7.1820, settled in Bathurst 30.10.1820. [PAO]

MCCUE, THOMAS, emigrated from Ireland to Canada on the Pitt 28.7.1820, settled in Bathurst 30.10.1820. [PAO]

MCCULLOUGH, HENRY, emigrated from Belfast on the St James, Captain Mark Collin, landed in Newcastle, Delaware, 22.7.1789. [Pa.Pkt.27.7.1789]

MCCULLOUGH, SAMUEL, emigrated from Belfast on the St James, Captain Mark Collin, landed in Newcastle, Delaware, 22.7.1789. [Pa.Pkt.27.7.1789]

MCDONALD, WILLIAM, emigrated from Newry on the brig Havannah, Captain Sutter, landed in Philadelphia 1.8.1789. [Pa.Pkt.6.8.1789]

MCELHINNEY, ROBERT, born 1747 and his wife Hannah born 1758, settled in Londonderry, Colchester County, Nova Scotia. [Folly Village g/s, N.S.]

MCFALL, JOHN, emigrated from Belfast on the St James, Captain Mark Collin, landed in Newcastle, Delaware, 22.7.1789. [Pa.Pkt.27.7.1789]

MCFARLANE, JAMES, emigrated from Londonderry on the Mary of Londonderry, Captain Cassidy, landed in Philadelphia 12.1789. [P.M.5.12.1789]

MCGEE, BERNARD, emigrated from Ireland to Canada on the Royal Edward 1819, settled in Beckwith 19.2.1821. [PAO]

MAGOWAN, SAMUEL, and family, emigrated from Belfast on the St James, Captain Mark Collin, landed in Newcastle, Delaware, 22.7.1789. [Pa.Pkt.27.7.1789]

MCILWRATH, ROBERT, emigrated from Belfast on the St James, Captain Mark Collin, landed in Newcastle, Delaware. 22.7.1789. [Pa.Pkt.27.7.1789]

MCJUNKIN, WILLIAM, emigrated from Londonderry on the Ann of Londonderry, master James Ramage, landed in Philadelphia 2.12.1785. [Pa.Pkt.6.12.1785]

MCKILLOP, WILLIAM, emigrated from Belfast on the St James, Captain Mark Collin, landed in Newcastle, Delaware, 22.7.1789. [Pa.Pkt.27.7.1789]

MCKIM, JOHN, born 1747, and his wife Ann born 1750, settled in Londonderry, Colchester County, Nova Scotia. [Folly Village g/s, N.S.]

MCKLENEN, BELL, born in Ireland 1797, with 3 children, arrived in Richmond on the schooner Emerald late 1821. [USNA]

MCKLENEN, F. born in Ireland 1793, a mason, arrived in Richmond on the schooner Emerald late 1821. [USNA]

MCKLENEN, LYDIA, born in Ireland 1793, arrived in Richmond on the schooner Emerald late 1821. [USNA]

MCKNEIGHT, ALEXANDER, and family, emigrated from Belfast on the St James, Captain Mark Collin, landed in Newcastle, Delaware, 22.7.1789. [Pa.Pkt.27.7.1789]

MCLEAN, ANDREW, emigrated from Newry on the brig Havannah, Captain Sutter, landed in Philadelphia 1.8.1789. [Pa.Pkt.6.8.1789]

MCLEAN, JOHN, emigrated from Belfast on the St James, Captain Mark Collin, landed in Newcastle, Delaware, 22.7.1789. [Pa.Pkt.27.7.1789]

MCLEAN, ROBERT, emigrated from Belfast on the St James, Captain Mark Collin, landed in Newcastle, Delaware, 22.7.1789. [Pa.Pkt.27.7.1789]

MCLELLAND, GEORGE, emigrated from Belfast on the St James, Captain Mark Collin, landed in Newcastle, Delaware, 22.7.1789. [Pa.Pkt.27.7.1789]

MCMAHAN, DANIEL, emigrated from Londonderry on the Ann of Londonderry, master James Ramage, landed in Philadelphia 2.12.1785. [Pa.Pkt.6.12.1785]

MCMAHON, JOSEPH, emigrated from Newry on the brig Havannah, Captain Sutter, landed in Philadelphia 1.8.1789. [Pa.Pkt.6.8.1789]

MCMASTER, JAMES, with his wife and son, emigrated from Ireland to Canada, settled in Bathurst 25.9.1820. [PAO]

MCMURRAY, JAMES, emigrated from Londonderry on the Nancy of Londonderry, master Thomas Crawford, landed at Newcastle, Delaware, 3.9.1789. [Pa.Pkt.7.11.1789]

MCNECK, NEIL, a laborer, born in Ireland 1800, with Sarah born in Ireland 1802, arrived in Alexandria late 1821 on the schooner Thetis, Captain Newcombe. [USNA]

MCNEELY, HUGH, emigrated from Londonderry on the Nancy of Londonderry, Captain Cassidy, landed in Philadelphia 12.1789. [P.M.5.12.1789]

MCNICKLE, GEORGE, emigrated from Londonderry on the Nancy of Londonderry, master Thomas Crawford, landed at Newcastle, Delaware, 3.9.1789. [Pa.Pkt.7.9.1789]

MCREE, DANIEL, emigrated from Belfast on the St James, Captain Mark Collin, landed in Newcastle, Delaware, 22.7.1789. [Pa.Pkt.27.7.1789]

MCSPADDAN, JOSEPH, with his wife, 3 sons and 3 daughters, emigrated from Ireland to Canada on the Eclipse 19.8.1817, settled in Elizabethtown 20.9.1817. [PAO]

MCSPADDAN, WILLIAM, and his wife, emigrated from Ireland to Canada on the Eclipse 19.8.1817, settled in Elizabethtown 20.9.1817. [PAO]

MCVEIGH, JAMES, emigrated from Belfast on the St James, Captain Mark Collin, landed in Newcastle, Delaware, 22.7.1789. [Pa.Pkt.27.7.1789]

MCWHINNIE, JOHN, with his wife and 2 sons, Donaghadie, emigrated from Ireland to Canda on the Alexander 20.6.1815, settled in Bathurst 19.7.1815. [PAO]

MAGHAN, THOMAS, emigrated from Newry on the brig Havannah, Captain Sutter, landed in Philadelphia 1.8.1789. [Pa.Pkt.6.8.1789]

MAHON, JAMES, emigrated from Ireland to Canada, settled in Drummond 18.10.1820. [PAO]

MALCOLM, MATTHEW, and wife, emigrated from Belfast on the St James, Captain Mark Collin, landed in Newcastle, Delaware, 22.7.1789. [Pa.Pkt.27.7.1789]

MANION, THOMAS, with his wife, 2 sons and a daughter, emigrated from Ireland to Canada, settled in Bathurst 15.6.1816. [PAO]

MARSHALL, HUGH, emigrated from Newry on the brig Havannah, Captain Sutter, landed in Philadelphia 1.8.1789. [Pa.Pkt.6.8.1789]

MARSHALL, JOHN, and family, emigrated from Belfast on the St James, Captain Mark Collin, landed in Newcastle, Delaware, 22.7.1789. [Pa.Pkt.27.7.1789]

MARTIN, Rev. JOHN, and son, emigrated from Belfast on the St James, Captain Mark Collin, landed in Newcastle, Delaware, 22.7.1789. [Pa.Pkt. 27.7.1789]

MARTIN, JOSEPH, emigrated from Belfast on the St James, Captain Mark Collin, landed in Newcastle, Delaware, 22.7.1789. [Pa.Pkt.27.7.1789]

MARTIN, WILLIAM, born in Ireland 1741, and his wife Ann born 1745, settled in Londonderry, Colchester County, Nova Scotia, by 1761. [Folly Village g/s, N.S.]

MATTHEWS, WILLIAM, emigrated from Londonderry on the Nancy of Londonderry, master Thomas Crawford, landed at Newcastle, Delaware, 3.9.1789. [Pa.Pkt.7.9.1789]

MAYNE, JOHN, emigrated from Belfast on the St James, Captain Mark Collin, landed in Newcastle, Delaware, 22.7.1789. [Pa.Pkt.27.7.1789]

MEAES, WILLIAM, emigrated from Londonderry on the Ann of Londonderry, master James Ramage, landed in Philadelphia 2.12.1785. [Pa.Pkt.6.12.1785]

MERCER, HENRY, emigrated from Belfast on the St James, Captain Mark Collin, landed in Newcastle, Delaware, 22.7.1789. [Pa.Pkt.27.7.1789]

MILIKEN, SAMUEL, emigrated from Belfast on the St James, Captain Mark Collin, landed in Newcastle, Delaware, 22.7.1789. [Pa.Pkt.27.7.1789]

MILLER, HUGH, emigrated from Belfast on the St James, Captain Mark Collin, landed in Newcastle, Delaware, 22.7.1789. [Pa.Pkt.27.7.1789]

MITCHELL, MARY, born in Ireland 1785, and her children, arrived in Alexandria on the schooner Emerald late 1821. [USNA]

MONTGOMERY, HENRY, with his wife, 2 sons and 3 daughters, County Tyrone, emigrated from Ireland to Canada on the Alexander 20.6.1815, settled in Bathurst 19.7.1815. [PAO]

MONTGOMERY, JAMES, emigrated from Londonderry on the Ann of Londonderry, master James Ramage, landed in Philadelphia 2.12.1785. [Pa.Pkt.6.12.1785]

MONTGOMERY, JAMES, County Tyrone, emigrated from Ireland to Canda on the Alexander 20.6.1815, settled in Bathurst 19.7.1815. [PAO]

MOORE, JOHN, and family, emigrated from Belfast on the St James, Captain Mark Collin, landed in Newcastle, Delaware, 22.7.1789. [Pa.Pkt.27.7.1789]

MOORE, RICHARD, emigrated from Londonderry on the brig Conyngham, master Robert Conyngham, landed in Newcastle, Delaware, 7.1789. [P.M.11.8.1789]

MORRIS, JAMES, with his wife and 5 sons, emigrated from Ireland to Canada on the Maria 29.6.1819, settled in Drummond 19.2.1821. [PAO]

MORRIS, THOMAS, with his wife, 2 sons and a daughter, emigrated from Ireland to Canada on the Mary and Ann 4.8.1817, settled in Marlborough 4.11.1817. [PAO]

MORRIS, WILLIAM, with his wife, son and 3 daughters, emigrated from Ireland to Canada on the Mary and Ann 4.8.1817, settled in Marlborough 4.11.1817. [PAO]

MORRISON, HUGH, emigrated from Londonderry on the Ann of Londonderry, master James Ramage, landed in Philadelphia 2.12.1785. [Pa.Pkt.6.12.1785]

MORRISON, WILLIAM, emigrated from Londonderry on the Ann of Londonderry, master James Ramage, landed in Philadelphia 2.12.1785. [Pa.Pkt.6.12.1785]

MORRON, JAMES, emigrated from Londonderry on the Nancy of Londonderry, master Thomas Crawford, landed at Newcastle, Delaware, 3.9.1789. [Pa.Pkt.7.9.1789]

MORRON, JOHN, emigrated from Londonderry on the Nancy of Londonderry, master Thomas Crawford, landed at Newcastle, Delaware, 3.9.1789. [Pa.Pkt.7.9.1789]

MORRON, RICHARD, emigrated from Londonderry on the Nanacy of Londonderry, master Thomas Crawford, landed at Newcastle, Delaware, 3.9.1789. [Pa.Pkt.7.9.1789]

MORRON, WILLIAM, emigrated from Londonderry on the Nancy of Londonderry, master Thomas Crawford, landed at Newcastle, Delaware, 3.9.1789. [Pa.Pkt.7.9.1789]

MORTON, JOHN, emigrated from Belfast on the St James, Captain Mark Collin, landed in Newcastle, Delaware, 22.7.1789. [Pa.Pkt.27.7.1789]

MORTON, WILLIAM, emigrated from Belfast on the St James, Captain Mark Collin, landed in Newcastle, Delaware, 22.7.1789. [Pa.Pkt.27.7.1789]

MOSSMAN, JOHN, sr. and family, emigrated from Belfast on the St James, Captain Mark Collin, landed in Newcastle, Delaware, 22.7.1789. [Pa.Pkt.27.7.1789]

MOSSMAN, JOHN, jr., and family, emigrated from Belfast on the St James, landed in Newcastle, Delaware, 27.7.1789. [Pa.Pkt.27.7.1789]

MULLINS, PATRICK, jr., emigrated from Ireland to Canada, settled in Dalhousie 8.11.1821. [PAO]

MURPHY, JAMES, with his wife, and 2 sons, emigrated from Ireland to Canada on the General Moore 8.8.1817, settled in Drummond 29.10.1817. [PAO]

MURPHY, MARY, born in Ireland 1783, with 2 children, arrived in Alexandria on the schooner Southern Trader, Captain Simpson, late 1821. [USNA]

MURRAY, JAMES, emigrated from Newry on the brig Havannah, Captain Sutter, landed in Philadelphia 1.8.1789. [Pa.Pkt.6.8.1789]

NICKLE, JAMES, emigrated from Belfast on the St James, Captain Mark Collin, landed in Newcastle, Delaware, 22.7.1789. [Pa.Pkt.27.7.1789]

NOLAN, HENRY, emigrated from Ireland to Canada on the Atlantic 27.6.1819, settled in Beckwith 25.9.1820. [PAO]

O'CLEARY, FRANCIS, emigrated from Londonderry on the Nancy of Londonderry, master Thomas Crawford, landed at Newcastle, Delaware, 3.9.1789. [Pa.Pkt.7.9.1789]

O'HARA, W.R., emigrated from Newry on the brig Havannah, Captain Sutter, landed in Philadelphia 1.8.1789. [Pa.Pkt.6.8.1789]

O'HARE, JAMES, with his wife, 3 sons and 1 daughter, emigrated from Ireland to Canada 11.1817, settled in Yonge 14.2.1818. [PAO]

O'NEILL, OWEN, emigrated from Newry on the brig Havannah, Captain Sutter, landed in Philadelphia 1.8.1789. [Pa.Pkt.6.8.1789]

OLIVER, ANDREW, emigrated from Ireland to Canada, settled in Dalhousie 9.11.1821. [PAO]

ORR, WILLIAM, emigrated from Londonderry on the Ann of Londonderry, master James Ramage, landed in Philadelphia 2.12.1785. [Pa.Pkt.6.12.1785]

OSBORNE, GEORGE, emigrated from Belfast on the St James, Captain Mark Collin, landed in Newcastle, Delaware, 22.7.1789. [Pa.Pkt.27.7.1789]

PARK, JAMES, emigrated from Belfast on the St James, Captain Mark Collin, landed in Newcastle, Delaware, 22.7.1789. [Pa.Pkt.27.7.1789]

PARKER, ANDREW, with his wife, 3 sons and 3 daughters, emigrated from Ireland to Canada on the Alexander 8.1820, settled in Bathurst 20.2.1821. [PAO]

PARKER, DAVID, emigrated from Ireland to Canada on the Alexander 8.1820, settled in Bathurst 20.2.1821. [PAO]

PARKINSON, ALEXANDER, and his wife, emigrated from Ireland to Canada on the Atlantic 14.8.1817, settled in Oxford 9.12.1817. [PAO]

PATTERSON, THOMAS, with his wife and daughter, emigrated from Ireland to Canada on the Eliza 1820, settled in Bathurst 9.9.1820. [PAO]

PATTON, CHARLES, emigrated from Londonderry on the Nancy of Londonderry, Captain Thomas Crawford, landed at Newcastle, Delaware, 3.9.1789. [Pa.Pkt.7.9.1789]

PEPPARD, LAURENCE, born in Ireland 1735, settled in Londonderry, Colchester County, Nova Scotia, by 1761. [Folly Village g/s, N.S.]

PERCIVAL, JOHN, and his wife, emigrated from Ireland to Canada on the Virginia 30.9.1817, settled in Landsdowne 23.12.1817. [PAO]

PERCIVAL, THOMAS, emigrated from Ireland to Canada on the Betty and Mary, 8.1.1818, settled in Landsdowne 21.2.1818. [PAO]

POLLOCK, JOHN, and family, emigrated from Belfast on the St James, Captain Mark Collin, landed in Newcastle, Delaware, 22.7.1789. [Pa.Pkt.27.7.1789]

POOLE, WILLIAM, emigrated from Ireland to Canada on the Atlantic 27.6.1819, settled in Drummond 25.9.1820. [PAO]

PURDUE, EDWARD, emigrated from Belfast on the St James, Captain Collin, landed in Newcastle, Delaware, 22.7.1789. [Pa.Pkt.27.7.1789]

QUIN, THOMAS, and his wife, emigrated from Ireland to Canada on the Jane 1819, settled in Bathurst 20.2.1821. [PAO]

RAMSEY, ROBERT, emigrated from Londonderry on the Ann of Londonderry, master James Ramage, landed in Philadelphia 2.12.1785. [Pa.Pkt.6.12.1785]

RAMSAY, WILLIAM, emigrated from Belfast on the St James, Captain Mark Collin, landed in Newcastle, Delaware, 22.7.1789. [Pa.Pkt.27.7.1789]

RATHWELL, SAMUEL, emigrated from Ireland to Canada on the Maria 29.6.1819, settled in Drummond 12.2.1821. [PAO]

REILLEY, JAMES, emigrated from Ireland to Canada on the Isabella 24.6.1820, settled in Bathurst 2.9.1820. [PAO]

RICHARDS, RICHARD, to Canada via USA, settled in Drummond 21.5.1817. [PAO]

RICHEY, STUART, emigrated from Londonderry on the Ann of Londonderry, master James Ramage, landed in Philadelphia 2.12.1785. [Pa.Pkt.6.12.1785]

RINGAN, JOHN, and family, emigrated from Belfast on the St James, Captain Mark Collin, landed in Newcastle, Delaware, 22.7.1789. [Pa.Pkt.27.7.1789]

RITCHARD, JOHN, emigrated from Londonderry on the Nancy of Londonderry, master Thomas Crawford, landed at Newcastle, Delaware, 3.9.1789. [Pa.Pkt.7.9.1789]

ROBINSON, HENRY, emigrated from Londonderry on the Nancy of Londonderry, Captain Cassidy, landed in Philadelphia 12.1789. [P.M.5.12.1789]

ROBINSON, THOMAS, with his wife and 4 daughters, County Down, emigrated from Ireland to Canada on the Alexander 20.6.1815, settled in Bathrst 19.7.1815. [PAO]

RUCKLE, HENRY, emigrated from Ireland to Canada, settled in Drummond 18.10.1820. [PAO]

RUTHWELL, BENJAMIN, with his wife and son, emigrated from Ireland to Canada on the John 19.9.1815, settled in Drummond 20.11.1815. [PAO]

RYAN, PATRICK, emigrated from Ireland to Canada, settled in Bathurst 25.9.1820. [PAO]

SALMON, THOMAS, and his wife, emigrated from Ireland to Canada on the Hannah 1820, settled in Bathurst 17.2.1821. [PAO]

SANDERSON, DANIEL, emigrated from Belfast on the St James, Captain Mark Collin landedin Newcastle, Delaware, 22.7.1789. [Pa.Pkt.27.7.1789]

SAYERS, ROBERT, emigrated from Londonderry on the Nancy of Londonderry, master Thomas Crawford, landed at Newcastle, Delaware, 3.9.1789. [Pa.Pkt.7.9.1789]

SCHOLFIELD, EDMOND, emigrated from Newry on the brig Havannah, Captain Sutter, landed in Philadelphia 1.8.1789. [Pa.Pkt.6.8.1789]

SCOTT, THOMAS, emigrated from Londonderry on the Nancy of Londonderry, Captain Cassidy, landed in Philadelphia 12.1789. [P.M.5.12.1789]

SCOTT, THOMAS, with his wife, son and 4 daughters, emigrated from Ireland to Canada on the Suffolk 8.6.1820, settled in Drummond 9.9.1820. [PAO]

SEABROOK, SARAH, born in Ireland 1789, a weaver, arrived in Alexandria on the ship Boston, Captain Fenly, late 1821.[USNA]

SHAW, THOMAS, emigrated from Londonderry on the Nancy of Londonderry, master Thomas Crawford, landed at Newcastle, Delaware, 3.9.1789. [Pa.Pkt.7.9.1789]

SHIELDS, THOMAS, emigrated from Belfast on the St James, Captain Mark Collin, landed in Newcastle, Delaware, 22.7.1789. [Pa.Pkt.27.7.1789]

SHORT, ARTHUR, emigrated from Belfast on the St James, Captain Mark Collin, landed in Newcastle, Delaware, 22.7.1789. [Pa.Pkt.27.7.1789]

SINGLETON, RICHARD, with his wife and daughter, emigrated from Ireland to Canada on the General Moore 20.8.1817, settled in Landsdowne 13.11.1817. [PAO]

SINGLETON, THOMAS, with his wife, 2 sons and 2 daughters, emigrated from Ireland to Canada on the General Moore 20.8.1817, settled in South Crosby 11.12.1817. [PAO]

SLY, WILLIAM, with wife, four sons and two daughters, to Canada on the Mary Ann, arrived 24.8.1817, settled in South Crosby 27.3.1818. [PAO]

SMITH, JOHN, emigrated from Belfast on the St James, Captain Mark Collin, landed in Newcastle, Delaware, 22.7.1789. [Pa.Pkt.27.7.1789]

SMITH, WILLIAM, emigrated from Londonderry on the Nancy of Londonderry, master Thomas Crawford landed at Newcastle, Delaware, 3.9.1789. [Pa.Pkt.3.9.1789. [Pa.Pkt.7.9.1789]

SMYLE, JOHN, emigrated from Belfast on the St James, Captain Mark Collin, landed in Newcastle, Delaware, 22.7.1789. [Pa.Pkt.27.7.1789]

SMYLE, WILLIAM, emigrated from Belfast on the St James, Captain Mark Collin, landed in Newcastle, Delaware, 22.7.1789. [Pa.Pkt.27.7.1789]

SNODDEN, THOMAS, and family, emigrated from Belfast on the St James, Captain Mark Collin, landed in Newcastle, Delaware, 22.7.1789. [Pa.Pkt.27.7.1789]

STEDMAN, JOSEPH, emigrated from Ireland to Canada, settled in Dalhousie 3.12.1821. [PAO]

STEDMAN, MICHAEL, emigrated from Ireland to Canada on the Mary and Bell 4.8.1817, settled in South Gower 30.11.1817. [PAO]

STEDMAN, NATHANIEL, with his wife, 2 sons and 5 daughters, emigrated from Ireland to Canada on the Mary and Bell 4.8.1817, settled in South Gower 30.11.1817. [PAO]

STEDMAN, THOMAS, and his wife, emigrated from Ireland to Canada on the Mary and Bell 4.8.1817, settled in South Gower 30.11.1817. [PAO]

STEEDMAN, FRANCIS, with wife, two sons and one daughter, emigrated from Ireland to Canada on the Mary and Bell, arrived 9.7.1818, settled in South Crosby 24.3.1818.[PAO]

STEPHENSON, JAMES, emigrated from Newry on the brig Havannah, Captain Sutter, landed in Philadelphia 1.8.1789. [Pa.Pkt.6.8.1789]

STEVENSON, DAVID, emigrated from Belfast on the St James, Captain Mark Collin, landed in Newcastle, Delaware, 22.7.1789. [Pa.Pkt.27.7.1789]

STEVENSON, JAMES, emigrated from Londonderry on the Ann of Londonderry, master James Ramage, landed in Philadelphia 2.12.1785. [Pa.Pkt.6.12.1785]

STEWART, ANDREW, emigrated from Londonderry on the Nancy of Londonderry, Captain Cassidy, landed at Philadelphia 12.1789. [P.M.5.12.1789]

STEWART, MARY, emigrated from Belfast on the St James, Captain Mark Collin, landed in Newcastle, Delaware, 22.7.1789. [Pa.Pkt.27.7.1789]

STEWART, ROBERT, emigrated from Newry on the brig Havannah, Captain Sutter, landed in Philadelphia 1.8.1789. [Pa.Pkt.6.8.1789]

STOTT, SAMUEL, emigrated from Belfast on the St James, Captain Mark Collin, landed in Newcastle, Delaware, 22.7.1789. [Pa.Pkt.27.7.1789]

SUMMERVILLE, JAMES, emigrated from Belfast on the St James, Captain Mark Collin, landed in Newcastle, Delaware, 22.7.1789. [Pa.Pkt.27.7.1789]

SUTTON, JOHN, emigrated from Ireland to Canada, settled in Lancaster 2.12.1821. [PAO]

SUTTON, Mrs, a widow, with her son, emigrated from Ireland to Canada, settled in Lancaster 29.11.1821. [PAO]

TACKLEBERRY, ANTHONY, and his wife, emigrated from Ireland to Canada, settled in Lancaster 9.11.1821. [PAO]

TACKLEBERRY, NATHANIEL, emigrated from Ireland to Canada, settled in Lancaster 9.11.1821. [PAO]

TATLOCK, JOHN, with his wife, 2 sons and 2 daughters, emigrated from Ireland to Canada on the John 19.9.1815, settled in Drummond 11.11.1815. [PAO]

TATLOCKE, WILLIAM, emigrated from Ireland to Canada, settled in Lancaster 3.12.1821. [PAO]

TAYLOR, ROBERT, emigrated from Newry on the brig Havannah, Captain Sutter, landed in Philadelphia 1.8.1789. [Pa.Pkt.6.8.1789]

TAYLOR, ROBERT, with his wife, 4 sons and 6 daughters, emigrated from Ireland to Canada on the General Moore 20.8.1817, settled in Landsdowne 28.11.1817. [PAO]

TAYLOR, ROBERT, jr., emigrated from Ireland to Canada on the General Moore 20.8.1817, settled in Landsdowne 28.11.1817. [PAO]

TEMPLETON, JOHN, (1), emigrated from Newry on the brig Havannah, Captain Sutter, landed in Philadelphia 1.8.1789. [Pa.Pkt.6.8.1789]

TEMPLETON, JOHN, (2), emigrated from Newry on the brig Havannah, Captain Sutter, landed in Philadelphia 1.8.1789. [Pa.Pkt.6.8.1789]

THOMSON, ANDREW, and family, emigrated from Belfast on the St James, Captain Mark Collin, landed in Newcastle, Delaware, 22.7.1789. [Pa.Pkt.27.7.1789]

THOMPSON, ANDREW, emigrated from Londonderry on the Nancy of Londonderry, Captain Cassidy, landed at Philadelphia 12.1789. [P.M.5.12.1789]

THOMPSON, JOSEPH, emigrated from Newry on the brig Havannah, Captain Sutter, landed in Philadelphia 1.8.1789. [Pa.Pkt.6.8.1789]

THOMPSON, ROBERT, (1), emigrated from Londonderry on the Nancy of Londonderry, master Thomas Crawford, landed at Newcastle, Delaware, 3.9.1789. [Pa.Pkt.7.9.1789]

THOMPSON, ROBERT, (2), emigrated from Londonderry on the Nancy of Londonderry, master Thomas Crawford, landed at Newcastle, Delaware, 3.9.1789. [Pa.Pkt.7.9.1789]

THOMPSON, SAMUEL, emigrated from Belfast on the St James, Captain Mark Collin, landed in Newcastle, Delaware, 22.7.1789. [Pa.Pkt.27.7.1789]

THOMPSON, WILLIAM, emigrated from Londonderry on the Nancy of Londonderry, Captain Cassidy, landed at Philadelphia 12.1789. [P.M.5.12.1789]

TOMPKINS, DENNIS, to Canada on the Mary Ann, arrived 8.8.1817, settled in Oxford 21.3.1818.[PAO]

TOPPING, EDWARD, with his wife and 4 daughters, County Down, emigrated from Ireland to Canada on the Alexander 20.6.1815, settled in Bathurst 19.7.1815. [PAO]

TRIMBLE, THOMAS, emigrated from Londonderry on the Nancy of Londonderry, master Thomas Crawford, landed at Newcastle, Delaware, 3.9.1789. [Pa.Pkt.7.9.1789]

TRUELAND, JAMES, emigrated from Londonderry on the Ann of Londonderry, master James Ramage, landed in Philadelphia 2.12.1785. [Pa.Pkt.6.12.1785]

TUCKINGTON, OLIVER, with 2 sons and 2 daughters, emigrated from Ireland to Canada on the Expedition 7.1818, settled in Sherbrooke 1.10.1820. [PAO]

VANCE, DAVID, born in Ireland 1748, and his wife Jane Hill born in Ireland 1755, settled in Londonderry, Colchester County, Nova Scotia, by 1761. [Folly Village g/s, N.S.]

VANCE, ELIZABETH, emigrated from Belfast on the St James, Captain Mark Collin, landed in Newcastle, Delaware, 22.7.1789. [Pa.Pkt.27.7.1789]

WAKEFIELD, DANIEL, emigrated from Londonderry on the Nancy of Londonderry, Captain Cassidy, landed in Philadelphia 12.1789. [P.M.5.12.1789]

WALKER, JOHN, with his wife and daughter, emigrated from Ireland to Canada on the Active 8.8.1817, settled in Kitley 17.12.1817. [PAO]

WARD, JAMES, emigrated from Ireland to Canada on the Hariot 28.6.1815, settled in Bathurst 14.10.1815. [PAO]

WARNER, JOSEPH, with hisw wife, 2 sons and 3 daughters, emigrated from Ireland to Canada on the General Moore 8.8.1817, settled in Landsdowne 21.10.1817. [PAO]

WARNOCK, JOHN, emigrated from Newry on the brig Havannah, Captain Sutter, landed in Philadelphia 1.8.1789. [Pa.Pkt.6.8.1789]

WARREN, WILLIAM, and wife, emigrated from Ireland to Canada on the Mary and Bell 23.8.1817, settled in Yonge Escott 17.10.1817. [PAO]

WATKINS, HENRY, emigrated from Ireland to Canada on the John 19.9.1815, settled in Drummond 6.11.1815. [PAO]

WATSON, ARCHIBALD, and family, emigrated from Belfast on the St James, Captain Mark Collin, landed in Newcastle, Delaware, 22.7.1789. [Pa.Pkt.27.7.1789]

WATSON, JAMES, emigrated from Newry on the brig Havannah, Captain Sutter, landed in Philadelphia 1.8.1789. [Pa.Pkt.6.8.1789]

WATSON, MATTHEW, emigrated from Londonderry on the Ann of Londonderry, master James Ramage, landed in Philadelphia 2.12.1785. [Pa.Pkt.6.12.1785]

WATSON, ROBERT, emigrated from Londonderry on the brig Conyngham, master Robert Conyngham, landed in Newcastle, Delaware, 7.1789. [P.M.11.8.1789]

WEST, CORNELIUS, emigrated from Newry on the brig Havannah, Captain Sutter, landed in Philadelphia 1.8.1789. [Pa.Pkt.6.8.1789]

WHAN, JAMES, emigrated from Belfast on the St James, Captain Mark Collin, landed in Newcastle, Delaware, 22.7.1789. [Pa.Pkt.27.7.1789]

WHITE, JAMES, and family, emigrated from Belfast on the St James, Captain Mark Collin, landed in Newcastle, Delaware, 22.7.1789. [Pa.Pkt.27.7.1789]

WHITELY, DANIEL, emigrated from Londonderry on the Nancy of Londonderry, master Thomas Crawford, landed at Newcastle, Delaware, 3.9.1789. [Pa.Pkt.7.9.1789]

WHITNEY, RICHARD, with his wife, 2 sons and 2 daughters, emigrated from Ireland to Canada on the Maria 29.6.1819, settled in bathurst 22.2.1821. [PAO]

WILLIAMSON, ALEXANDER, emigrated from Belfast on the St James, Captain Mark Collin, landed in Newcastle, Delaware, 22.7.1789. [Pa.Pkt.27.7.1789]

WILLIS, GEORGE, emigrated from Belfast on the St James, Captain Mark Collin, landed in Newcastle, Delaware, 22.7.1789. [Pa.Pkt.27.7.1789]

WILLOCK, JOHN, wife and three daughters, to Canada on the Harriet, arrived 28.8.1817, settled in Leeds 13.4.1818. [PAO]

WILSON, ADAM, and wife, emigrated from Belfast on the St James, Captain Mark Collin, landed in Newcastle, Delaware, 22.7.1789. [Pa.Pkt.27.7.1789]

WILSON, ELIZA, emigrated from Belfast on the St James, Captain Mark Collin, landed in Newcastle, Delaware, 22.7.1789. [Pa.Pkt.27.7.1789]

WILSON, JAMES, sr., with his wife and 2 daughters, County Down, emigrated from Ireland to Canada on the Alexander 20.6.1815, settled in Bathurst 19.7.1815. [PAO]

WILSON, JAMES, jr., County Down, emigrated from Ireland to Canada on the Alexander 20.6.1815, settled in Bathurst 19.7.1815. [PAO]

WILSON, JOHN, emigrated from Londonderry on the Nancy of Londonderry, master Thomas Crawford, landed at Newcastle, Delaware, 3.9.1789. [Pa.Pkt.7.9.1789]

WILSON, JOSEPH, and family, emigrated from Belfast on the St James, Captain Mark Collin, landed in Newcastle, Delaware, 22.7.1789. [Pa.Pkt.27.7.1789]

WILSON, SAMUEL, emigrated from Belfast on the St James, Captain Mark Collin, landed in Newcastle, Delaware, 22.7.1789. [Pa.Pkt.27.7.1789]

WRIGHT, MOSES, emigrated from Belfast on the St James, Captain Mark Collin, landed in Newcastle, Delaware, 22.7.1789. [Pa.Pkt.27.7.1789]

WRIGHT, SAMUEL, and wife, to Canada on the Mary and Bell , arrived 9.7.1817, settled in Lansdowne 1.4.1818. [PAO]

YOUNG, ANDREW, emigrated from Belfast on the St James, Captain Mark Collin, landed in Newcastle, Delaware, 22.7.1789. [Pa.Pkt.27.7.1789]

YOUNG, GEORGE, emigrated from Belfast on the St James, Captain Mark Collin, landed in Newcastle, Delaware, 22.7.1789. [Pa.Pkt.27.7.1789]

YOUNG, GEORGE, with his wife, 2 sons and 2 daughters, emigrated from Ireland to Canada on the Hopewell 3.9.1817, settled in Oxford 13.10.1817. [PAO]

YOUNG, GEORGE, emigrated from Ireland to Canada on the Brown 19.7.1819, settled in Drummond 9.9.1820. [PAO]

YOUNG, JOHN, and son, emigrated from Belfast on the St James, Captain Mark Collin, landed in Newcastle, Delaware, 22.7.1789. [Pa.Pkt.27.7.1789]

YOUNG, THOMAS, jr., and his wife and daughter, emigrated from Ireland to Canada on the Mary and Bell 8.7.1817, settled in South Gower 31.10.1817. [PAO]

REFERENCES

GG = "Roll of Graduates of the University of Glasgow, 1727-1898" W.I.Addison, [Glasgow, 1898]
Pa.Pkt = Pennsylvania Packet and Daily Advertiser
P.M. = Pennsylvania Mercury
PAO = Public Archives of Ontario
USNA = United States National Archives